introduction by neil gaiman

YEAR'S BEST GRAPHIC NOVELS COMICS & MANGA

from Blankets to Demo to Blacksad

edited by byron preiss and howard zimmerman

Edited by BYRON PREISS
and HOWARD ZIMMERMAN

Introduction by NEIL GAIMAN

St. Martin's Griffin New York

DEDICATED TO
THE MEMORY AND VISION
OF BYRON PREISS
1953 - 2005

THE YEAR'S BEST GRAPHIC NOVELS, COMICS, AND MANGA.

For information, address St. Martin's Press, 175 Fifth Avenue, New York, N.Y. 10010.

Edited by Byron Preiss and HOWARD ZIMMERMAN
Project Coordinator MAUREEN MCTIGUE
Cover design by DEAN MOTTER
Interior design by ARNIE SAWYER

Special thanks to
Christopher Butcher, Jennifer Contino, Jake T. Forbes, Heidi MacDonald and Greg McElhatton
The Guys at Komikwerks.com

Thanks to Shalema McGhee, Max Ulanoff, April Issacs, Paul Levitz, Richard Bruning, Dan Vado, Jennifer de Guzman, Kim Thompson, Eric Reynolds, James Lucas Jones, Chris Staros, Brett Warnock, Eric Shanower, Jim Ottoviani, Steve Leiber, Jeremy Ross, Eric Stephenson, Matt Forsythe, Ted Adams, Neil Kleid, Evelyn Dubocq, Jamie Quail, Peggy Burns, Anders Nilsen, Jessica Able, Larry Young, Chris Pitzer, Paul Hornschemeir, Paul Rivoche, Mark Smylie, Sean Stewart, Steve Bryant, Larry Daley, Allen Hui, and Mark and the gang at Cosmic Comics

For individual copyrights, please see page 270-272.

A BYRON PREISS BOOK

www.stmartins.com

Library of Congress Cataloging-in-Publication Data
Year's Best Graphic Novels, Comics & Manga/edited by Byron Preiss and Howard Zimmerman.
p. cm. "Byron Preiss book."
ISBN: 0-312-34326-4 (pbk)
ISNB-13: 978-0-312-34326-2
ISBN: 0-312-34325-6 (hc)
ISBN-13: 978-0-312-34325-5

1. Graphic Novels

First Edition: December 2005

10 9 8 7 6 5 4 3 2 1

Foreword..........

By Editor Howard Zimmerman

This volume is the result of the combined vision of Marc Resnick, editor at St. Martin's Press and genuine comic-book fan, and the late Byron Preiss, genuine comic-book visionary. And the combined labors of ace co-editor Maureen McTigue and designers Dean Motter and Arnie Sawyer.

The goal of this volume is to expose comics fans to worthwhile areas of the field they may not have yet experienced. Those who spend the majority of their comics-reading time with superheroes will discover that tights-and-fights are not the only enjoyable reads available. Those who focus their attention on Manga should be pleased to see that there are many, many different kinds of stories and formats now available to them. In fact, the comics field is probably more diverse and richer in talent than it has ever been before. And we've drawn work from almost two dozen publishers, independent presses, and self-owned-and-published comics to prove it.

All publishers were invited to participate. Unfortunately, Marvel Comics and Dark Horse Comics declined for their own reasons. Hopefully, they will reconsider and be a presence in next year's volume. And, because of a combination of space limitations and time constraints, such landmark publications as *Cerebus* #300 and the final *Bone* saga are not here, either. Which brings up the question: If it's not here, does that mean it's not among the year's best? And the answer is: Of course not. It would have taken a multi-volume, several-thousand-page series to fully represent the wonderful output of creators and publishers during the past year. Well, not exactly the past year. Given the realities of book publishing, we could not be up to the minute or all-inclusive.

introduction by neil gaiman
YEAR'S
BEST
from Blankets to Demo to Blacksad
GRAPHIC
NOVELS
COMICS
&
MANGA
edited by byron preiss and howard zimmerman

Selections were made from publications that appeared during the period of May 2003 to December 2004. We've parsed down this enormous volume of creative work into three main categories and a fourth catch-all:

During the course of reading through suggested entries, I rediscovered my love for superhero stories, told well by mature creative teams, and had my eyes opened by the fine work of today's burgeoning field of independent comics producers and self-publishers. I was particularly impressed with *Batman: Hush* and Carla Speed McNeil's work on *Queen and Country*, to name just two.

In addition to reproducing excerpts and cover art from dozens and dozens of periodicals and books, we've also briefly covered the area of web-based comics, where the work keeps getting better and better, stories from comics' anthologies, and several short works. The lengths of the excerpts were driven by several considerations, such as the length of the entire work and the number of entries in that category.

Read on: the thrill of discovery awaits.

Introduction........

By Neil Gaiman

Award-winning, best-selling author and comics writer Neil Gaiman presented this speech in a longer form as the keynote address at the June 2004 Harvey Awards, one of the premiere ceremonies in the comics community.

When, as a young man, my dream of getting to make comics started to become a reality, I started to meet comics people. These were the people who I had looked up to in my teens, in my twenties, as gods upon the earth. These were the names that I conjured with. I would read everything I could about them when I was growing up, in a time when there was precious little about them to read, and even less of what they had done still in print.

And now I was to meet them.

And I discovered, to my surprise, that quite a lot of them were cranky old Jews. Or wannabe cranky old Jews—they seemed to be enjoying themselves too much to be properly cranky, and not all of them were actually Jewish.

And now, approaching my mid-forties, eighteen years after writing my first comic, I find myself heading down the conveyor belt towards cranky old Jewhood. I'm at the age where they start to give you lifetime achievement awards, and you rather wish they wouldn't, because it may be some kind of a hint that it's time for you to sit down and shut up.

It is the prerogative, however, of those who are one day to be cranky old Jews to give advice to the generations that will follow them. And while some of you are my contemporaries, and others are my seniors, I shall advise anyway. My first piece of advice is this:

Ignore all advice.

In my experience, most interesting art gets made by people who don't know the rules, and have no idea that certain things simply aren't done: so they do them. Transgress. Break things. Have too much fun.

2) Read outside of comics. Learn from places that aren't comics. Don't do what anyone else is doing. Steal from places that people aren't looking. Go outside. Many years ago, when it was almost unheard of for foreigners to write American comics, people used to ask why British Writers were different. I had no idea. I did notice that when I spoke socially to people like Alan Moore, or to Grant Morrison, we mostly weren't talking about comics. We were talking about avant garde forms of poetry, about non-fiction writers, about weird things we'd found. Grant Morrison discovered a long-forgotten Victorian children's author named Lucy Clifford, who wound up influencing both his *Doom Patrol* and, much later, my *Coraline*. We loved comics, but they weren't all we knew. There's a whole cool world out there. Use it.

3) Read all the comics you can. Know your comics.

The history of comics is not a long one, and it's not unknowable. We can argue about whether or not hieroglyphics were the earliest comics, or the Bayeux tapestry or what. At the end of the day, we don't have a long history. You can learn it. You can, these days more easily that you ever could before, study it. And the high points of the last century in comics are quite astonishing. There are things that Winsor McCay did in *Little Nemo* that are still unsurpassed. Things in Herriman's *Krazy Kat* that are jaw dropping. There are things, as a writer and as a storyteller, that Harvey Kurtzman did, that Will Eisner did, that Robert Crumb did that you should familiarize yourself with and learn from.

There's more classic and important material in print now in affordable editions than there has ever been. Let it inspire you. See how high people have taken the medium in the past, and resolve to take it further.

Isaac Newton, even as he created the foundations of huge swatches of science, said that if he had seen a little further than most men, it was because he was standing on the shoulders of giants.

We've inherited an art form from giants, some of whom were cranky old Jews, and some of whom weren't Jews, and some of whom weren't even cranky.

Another piece of advice:

I've learned over the years that everything is more or less the same amount of work, so you may as well set your sights high and try and do something really cool.

There are other people around who can do the mediocre, meat-and-potatoes work that anybody can do. So let them do that. You make the art that only you can make. You tell the stories only you can tell.

As a solution to various problems you may encounter upon the way, let me suggest this:

Make Good Art.

It's very simple. But it seems to work. Life fallen apart? Make good art. True love ran off with the milkman? Make good art. Bank foreclosing? Make good art.

Keep moving, learn new skills. Enjoy yourself.

Most of the work I've done that's been highly regarded has happened in places where, when I was working on it I tended to suspect that it would go one of two ways – either I was doing something cool that, if I was lucky, people would talk about for some time, or I was doing something that people would have a particularly good laugh about, in the places where they gather to discuss the embarrassing mistakes of those who went before them.

Be proud of your mistakes. Well, proud may not be exactly the right word, but respect them, treasure them, be kind to them, learn from them.

And, more than that, and more important than that, make them.

Make mistakes. Make great mistakes, make wonderful mistakes, make glorious mistakes. Better to make a hundred mistakes than to stare at a blank piece of paper too scared to do anything wrong, too scared to do anything.

Critics will grumble. Of course they will. That's one of the functions of critics. As an artist it's your job to give them ulcers, and perhaps even something to get apoplectic about.

Most of the things I've got right over the years, I got right because I'd got them wrong first. It's how we make art.

As a keynote speaker for the Eisners [in 2003] I said that compared to where I dreamed that comics could be, as a young journalist in 1986, we're in a Golden Age.

And I was taken to task in certain circles for this, as if I'd said that this was as good as things could get, or that there was nothing at all wrong with the world of comics. Obviously neither statement is true.

We're in 2004, the year that Dave Sim and Gerhard finished the 300 issues of *Cerebus*, the year that Jeff Smith completed *Bone*, both monumental tasks, both unique. *Cerebus* cannot be compared with anything anyone else has done. It's unparalleled in its evolving portrait of its subject and its subject's creator. *Bone* is, beginning to end, the best fantasy tale anyone's told in comics. That in itself gives me hope for the future.

It's the year that my daughter Maddy discovered *Bettie and Veronica*, and that gives me another kind of hope. Any world in which a nine year old girl can become, off her own bat, a mad keen comics collector because she cares about the stories, is a good one.

I think the Internet is changing things.

Twice in the last eighteen months the Internet has been used as a way of rallying around publishers who needed help. Good publishers who had cash flow problems, and who put out appeals for assistance, letting people know that now was the time to buy. And people did. The Internet meant that information was given to the people who needed it.

Last week, a web-cartoonist with a large readership, who had told his readership that he would really like to quit his day job and devote the time to the comic, if they could raise the same money he made in his day job. His readers dipped into their pockets, five dollars here and ten dollars there, and delivered the annual wages from his day job.

The Internet gives your comics cheap access to the world, without printing bills. Of course, it still hasn't worked out a reliable way to pay people for their work, but Randy Milholland quit his job yesterday to do *Something Positive* full-time, and Top Shelf and Fantagraphics are both still here.

Despite the grumblers, I think the Internet is a blessing, not a curse.

And if I have a prediction it's simply this: the often-predicted Death of Comics won't happen. There will be more booms and there will be more busts. Fads and fashions turn up in comics, as with all things, and, as fads and fashions always do, they end, normally in tears.

But comics is a medium, not a fad. It's an art form, not a fashion. The novel was once so called because it was indeed something novel, but it's lasted, and I think, after a few shakedowns, the graphic novel, in whatever form, will do likewise.

Already some things are changing:

When I started writing about comics, before I ever began to write comics, I wanted a world in which comics would simply be regarded as a medium like any other, and in which we were accorded the same respect that any other medium was given. The amount of respect that novels and films and great works of art got. I wanted us to get literary awards. I wanted comics to turn up on the shelves of bookshops, and to sit next to books on the bestseller lists. Maybe one day a comic could come out and be on the *New York Times* bestseller list.

We've got all that. And I don't think it's important after all.

Right now I actually believe that the best thing about comics may well be that it is a gutter medium. We do not know which fork to use, and we eat with our fingers. We are creators of a medium, we create art in an art form, which is still alive, which is powerful, which can do things no other medium can do.

I don't believe that a fraction of the things that can be done with comics have yet been done.

For now, I think we've barely scratched the surface.

And I think that's exciting. I don't know where comics as a medium will go in the future. But I want to be amazed, and I'm pretty sure that I shall be.

And I trust that one day when you, whatever age, race, gender, or ethnicity you may lay claim to, are in your turn a cranky old Jew up here giving a speech, that that will always remain true.

introduction by neil gaiman
YEAR'S BEST
from Blankets to Demo to Blacksad
GRAPHIC NOVELS
COMICS & MANGA
edited by byron preiss and howard zimmerman

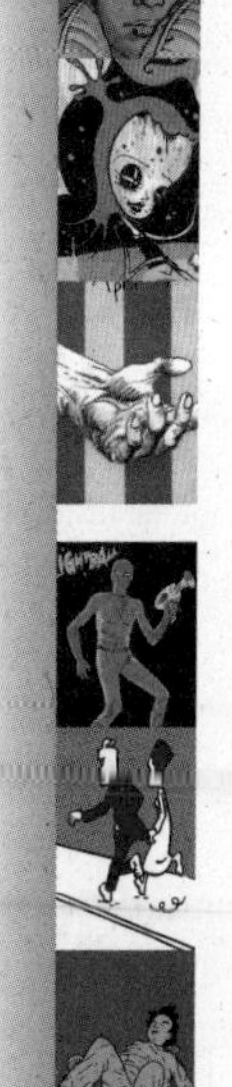

Graphic Novels

By Heidi MacDonald

The timing couldn't be better, really. This inaugural edition of The Year's Best Graphic Novels comes at a time when the form has reached a critical mass much predicted. Setting aside marketing worries that have long preoccupied great minds, the creators of the books gathered here have simply reveled in the power of a medium to tell stories. If there was any doubt that comics—to call them by their dirty, pulp name—are a medium of endless invention, here is the proof.

At one end, baroque tales explore comics' pulp origins. Alan Moore and Kevin O'Neill take familiar heroes and reinvent them with *League of Extraordinary Gentlemen*, while Mark Smylie delivers epic fantasy in a sumptuous style in *Artesia*.

Comics' continuing fascination with hardboiled heroes gets explored in radically different ways. Greg Rucka's spy, Tara Chace, shows her vulnerability in *Queen and Country*. In *Last of the Independents* by Matt Fraction and Keiron Dwyer, one last heist goes wrong, with sepia art paying homage to caper-film roots. *Blacksad* by Juan Diaz Canales and Juanjo Guarnido takes every hardboiled cliché and adds spectacular art and a cast of animals.

Funny animals, a mainstay of comics from *Krazy Kat* to Snoopy, prove that they can be radically unfunny in Jason's extraordinary *You Can't Get There From Here*. Just to prove how different animal characters can be there's *Owly*, Andy Runton's charming little owl.

Moving into art for art's sake, there's *Blab!*, Monte Beauchamp's long running explosion of pop culture sensibility. Bridging the gap between art and story–and showing how far "art" comics have come–there's Anders Nilssen's haunting *Dogs and Water*, a dreamlike tale of a boy and a stuffed bear wandering a wasteland.

Comics have always been a place for the coming-of-age story, and the many directions that theme can go. In *Superman: Secret Identity*, Kurt Busiek and Stuart Immonen take the hoariest of comic book tales and give it human dimension. Dave Gibbons takes his own Mod youth and projects it into *The Originals*, a grim, dystopian future where individuality is a life or death proposition. In the delightful *Scott Pilgrim's Precious Little Life*, Bryan Lee O'Malley pokes fun at his own generation's lack of purpose to make the sitcom no network would dare. Craig Thompson's multi-award winning *Blankets* is a story of first love story that few can resist.

Finally, there are non-fiction comics. In *Suspended in Language* by Jim Ottaviani and Leland Purvis, quantum physics and history come to vivid life with the story of physicist Niels Bohr. Joe Kubert, legendary comics artist, takes on one of the harshest events of human history, with *Yossel*, the story of the doomed Warsaw Ghetto Uprising.

The year's best graphic novels present endless worlds to explore, from campy heroics to fractured fairy tales to the blasted streets of Sarajevo, from Shakespearean superheroes to Victorian mass murderers. Surveying the pleasures to be had here, there is no need for apology or explanation. Just dive right in and see for yourself.

Graphic

Table of Contents

UH, HELLO?
WE NEED AN AMBULANCE--I'M NOT SURE WHERE WE ARE. SOMEWHERE IN NORTH JERSEY...
I CAN'T-- CAN'T BELIEVE IT...
There were broken bones, both from the spin and the hurried landing. But they'd all be okay. And I'm pretty sure nobody saw me.

Not that it'd matter if they did.

That's why I wear the costume. I learned years ago that if people knew about me, I'd have no peace. I'd be a freak, a curiosity. A monster, even.

kurt busiek stuart immonen

SUPERMAN secret identity

People would go nuts--wanting to know how I can do it, where the powers come from.

And I don't even know any of that myself.

But if someone sees me, what are they going to say?

"It was Superman, officer. He swooped out of the sky and saved me!"

Yeah, sure. Who's going to believe that? I've seen some stories on the Internet, stuff I've done. Everyone treats it as a joke.

No, as long as I don't get spotted right out in broad daylight, I'm safe.

SUPERMAN: SECRET IDENTITY (DC Comics)

I'm safe.
BLUE REMOTE TO BLUE BASE. WE HAVE ANOTHER CONFIRMED.
NO WORKABLE PRINTS--BUT THERE ARE FINGER GOUGES IN THE METAL. AND FOOTPRINTS--DEEP FOOTPRINTS--NOT ACCOUNTED FOR.
YESSIR. SITE SECURED. COLLECTION TEAM EN ROUTE.

But it bothers me a little. It used to be more fun.
Just knowing I could do all this, that I was special. It was my secret. My one rare truth, that I knew and nobody else did.
I still like it--I love the flying, I'm glad I can save lives. I'd never give it up.

But something's missing.
KENT! MITTELMARK WANTS YOU IN HER OFFICE. NOW.
HUH?

UH, MA'AM?
AH, CLARK. COME IN, COME IN.

STILL CAN'T GET OVER THAT.
CLARK KENT. FROM SMALLVILLE, KANSAS, AND YOU'RE A JOURNALIST.
NOT REALLY, MA'AM.
HM?

I'M A *WRITER,* BUT I DON'T WANT TO BE A REPORTER. AND I'M FROM *PICKETSVILLE.*
SURE, SURE.
UH, DID I DO SOMETHING *WRONG?*

HM? NO, YOUR STAFF WORK IS FINE. I WANT TO TALK ABOUT THIS NEW *PIECE* YOU SUBMITTED.
POPULATION DENSITY AS A MEDIUM FOR BOTH *CULTURAL FERMENT* AND *SOCIETAL DECAY.* INTERESTING. *WELL-OBSERVED.*
I'VE MARKED A FEW SPOTS WHERE THE PROSE IS *UNCLEAR,* BUT I THINK WE CAN BUY IT.

THANK YOU. THAT'S--
YOU HAVE AN UNUSUAL *PERSPECTIVE,* KENT. LIKE YOU SEE THE WORLD FROM *OUTSIDE*--AS A DETACHED OBSERVER, NOT AS A PARTICIPANT.
UH, THANKS *AGAIN.* I TRY TO--

IT WASN'T *WHOLLY* A COMPLIMENT. YOUR WORK ESCAPES *DRYNESS,* BUT STILL, IT'S ALL *HEAD,* NO HEART.
YOU NEED TO GET *OUT* THERE, MIX IT UP. GET *INVOLVED* IN LIFE. GET YOUR HEART BROKEN, GET *LAID. FEEL,* AS WELL AS THINK.

UH...
STILL...
...ADAM BILMES AT PANTHEON LIKED YOUR EARLIER PIECE, ABOUT GRIDLOCK AS A METAPHOR FOR *INTERNATIONAL DIPLOMACY.*
HE ASKED FOR AN ADVANCE LOOK AT *THIS* ONE. HE'D LIKE TO TALK--SEE IF YOU HAVE A *BOOK* IN YOU.
GIVE HIM A *CALL.*
HE...A *BOOK?*

SUPERMAN: SECRET IDENTITY (DC Comics)

I thought I was going to be fired. Instead, I've got a lunch next Tuesday with a senior editor at Pantheon.
He wants to hear book ideas. Book ideas!
I guess I was still reeling from that--

RISTORANTE ROSSI
--and when the guys suggested we all go out for beers and a burger after work, I didn't think.
Didn't realize what they were up to.

AH, *HERE* SHE IS.
CLARK--

--MEET **LOIS.**
OH, **CHRIST.** NOT **ANOTHER** ONE.
WHAT?

HA HA HA HA HA HA HA HA
GREAT, YOU'VE **HAD** YOUR JOKE. YOU'LL **PAY,** LINDSEY.
HAVE A HELL OF A **NIGHT.**

NICE **WORK** THERE, GUYS. REAL **MATURE.**
AW, **C'MON,** CLARK--

HEY, IT'S **ME.** LOOK, I'D LIKE TO **APOLOGIZE** FOR--
YEAH, YEAH, IT WAS ALL JUST **HARMLESS FUN,** RIGHT?
LISTEN, IF YOU KNEW HOW MANY **TIMES** I'VE--

--NO, WAIT. YOU PROBABLY DO, HUH?
PROBABLY. I'M NOT JUST A CLARK. I'M A CLARK KENT.
I'VE BEEN SET UP WITH EIGHTEEN LOISES, SEVEN LANAS, AND A CAT GRANT.

CAT GRANT? IS THAT SOMEONE FROM SUPERMAN?
BEATS ME. MY COLLEGE ROOMMATE THOUGHT IT WAS HYSTERICAL, THOUGH, SO I GUESS SO.

W 42

SORRY IF I WAS RUDE.
NO PROBLEM. I'D DO THAT MYSELF, IF I HAD THE GUTS.

HI. CLARK KENT. BUT YOU KNEW THAT.
HI. LOIS CHAUDHARI.

LOOK, I'M GUESSING YOU DON'T HAVE DINNER PLANS. MINE JUST FELL THROUGH TOO, SO IF YOU'D LIKE TO...
LOOK, NO OFFENSE, BUT--
AH, WHAT THE HELL. YOU SEEM NICE ENOUGH.
JUST PROMISE ME YOU DON'T HAVE A FRIEND NAMED LEX, WHO'S GOING TO KIDNAP ME AND THREATEN THE CITY WITH HIS DEATH RAY.
2 FIST
WHIP

I mentioned before how much I'm liking Manhattan. Especially at night.
So just let me add this:
It's way, way better when you're sharing it with someone.
She's working for an interior designer. She likes it a lot.
--ALWAYS LIKED TO WRITE, BUT WITH THIS NAME, I FIGURE NO NEWSPAPERS. NOT FOR ME.
She's from San Francisco. Went to Carleton College in Minnesota.
She loves Joel Garreau's books too. And she knows Tevis--she's even read The Queen's Gambit!
She wants to go around the world in a balloon someday.
Her nose wrinkles up when she laughs.
And she smiles--
--she smiles like life's a joke, and you're in on it with her.

SO, HOW'D WE DO? WORTH ANOTHER TRY SOMETIME?
I'LL HAVE TO GIVE YOU A BUZZ ON THE OL' SIGNAL WATCH SOMETIME.
THAT'S JIMMY OLSEN.
WHATEVER.
If I sound smitten, don't read too much into it--

SUPERMAN: SECRET IDENTITY (DC Comics)

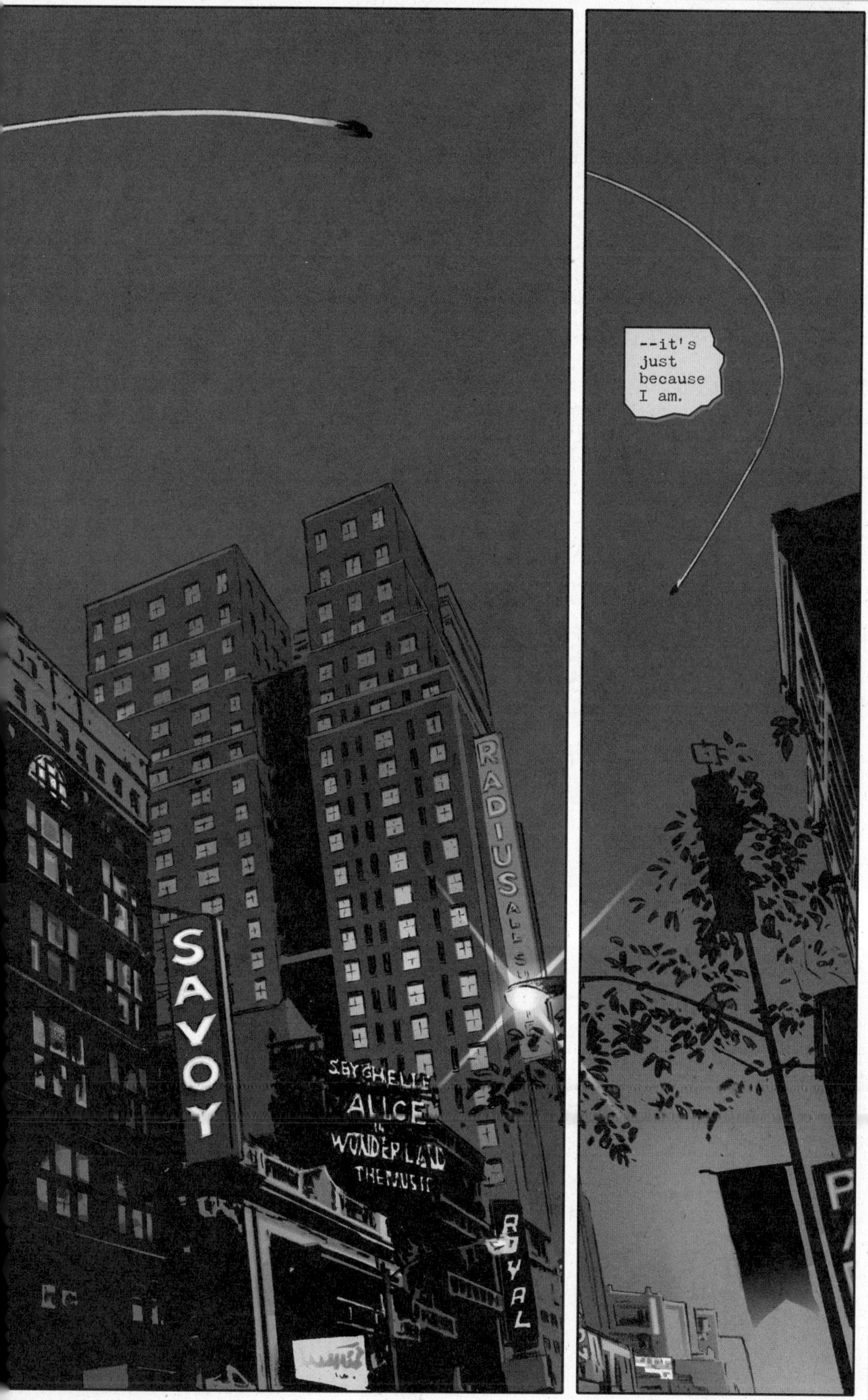

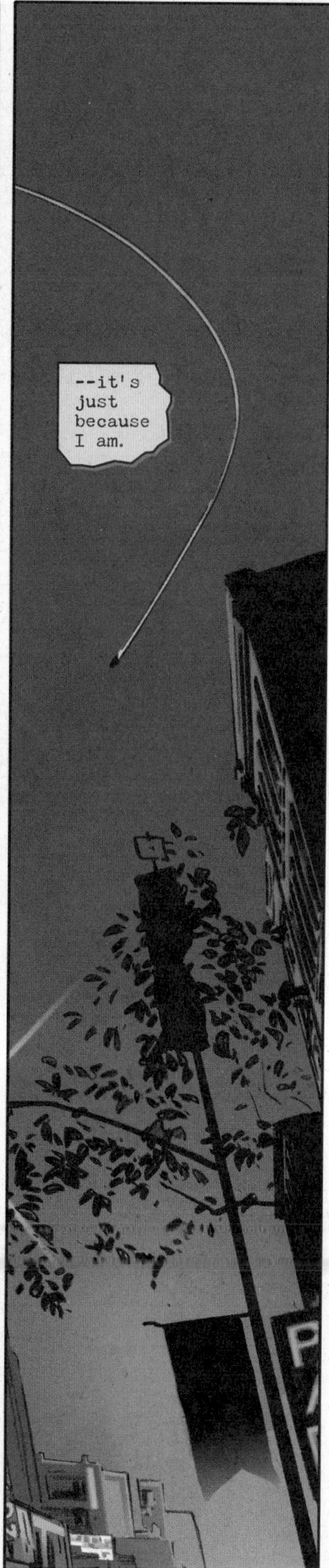
--it's just because I am.

SUPERMAN: SECRET IDENTITY (DC Comics)

So when I was a kid,

and my brother and I shared a bed,

We loved to pretend the bed was a boat,

and the floor was endless stretches of ocean...

Blankets

an illustrated novel by
CRAIG THOMPSON

BLANKETS (Top Shelf Productions)

We'd gather all our stuffed animals together--
ARR
AHOY
--and pitch a bedsheet for a sail.
And then came the fun part...
What?

BLANKETS (Top Shelf Productions)

BLANKETS (Top Shelf Productions)

Inevitably, a storm would strike and do a number on our ship.

CRUSH the bow,

SHATTER the poop deck,

FLING one bean-stuffed pirate to his fate,

GSSSH

and FINALLY leave our bed coverings in a state of disarray.

Then we'd gather those crumpled blankets, salvage any remaining crewmates, and wind a nest about us.
The storm would persist all night with waves sloshing the boat and rain gushing down overhead,
But in that little pathetic clump of blankets, there was comfort.
CHSSSHHH
HHHHHHHHHHHH
Z

Those were some of the only times I enjoyed sharing a bed with him.
Aww...
Well, when I was a little girl...
..., I'd use my parents' bed (because it was so big) to host an elaborate banquet.
I'd fold one blanket up nice and evenly--
FOR A TABLE...

BLANKETS (Top Shelf Productions)

...And surround it with pillows--

FOR CHAIRS.

For dinner, I'd sort through a box of plastic ingredients...

PLAYSKOOL

...and arrange UNIQUE servings:

PIE and an EGG

T-BONE and BANANA

If I was desperate, I'd offer STRAWBERRY SHORTCAKE up for sacrifice.

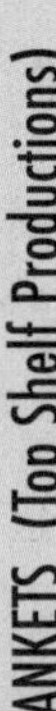
BLANKETS (Top Shelf Productions)

Unfortunately, none of my invitees were stuffed animals.
Ben and Lauren always showed up; Julie always declined.
And an additional family member at that time was--
-- I kid you not --
-- A PET MONKEY.
HA HA! As if your household wasn't already a ZOO!
No. I'm serious. He was a CINNAMON CAPUCHIN--
--and his name was "SNOWBALL".
So he was WHITE?

BLANKETS (Top Shelf Productions)

No, It's just a cute name little girls pick for their pets.
Ben was always a perfect dinner guest--politely enjoying his food.
Lauren just sort of smiled and watched.
But SNOWBALL never stayed in place.

THROWING--
--Stealing--
Give it
BONK
YANK
--and Finally dismantling the entire table.

BLANKETS (Top Shelf Productions)

HA HA! That's great!
So what'll it be tonight?

BLANKETS (Top Shelf Productions)

"Dinner" or "shipwreck"?

The way she asked questions like that!

both.

It's starting to rain.

BLANKETS (Top Shelf Productions)

PEACE ON EARTH
GRAND NEW DIORAMA
BUY ANTI-STIFF
MEN FROM MARS BEHAVE LIKE HUN

I MUST CONFESS, I ADMIRE THE BRITISH PEOPLE'S **BRAVERY**. WITH HORROR AT THEIR DOORSTEP, THEY SEEM **UNCONCERNED**.
Huh. HARDLY UNCONCERNED. MORE **BLINKERED**, I'D HAVE SAID.
PRETENDING EVERYTHING'S TICKETY-BOO, NEMO. IT'S THE GREAT BRITISH **PASTIME**.

ALAN MOORE · KEVIN O'NEILL · The LEAGUE of EXTRAORDINARY GENTLEMEN · VOLUME II

OUR **DRIVER'S** A DAMNED COWARD, I KNOW THAT MUCH. REFUSING TO GO NEAR THAT SLUG-PIT...
ON THE CONTRARY. HEARING HIM SPEAK TO YOU, I DID NOT THINK HIM COWARDLY.

HOLMES SAID SAMSON WAS A *MAHDI* VETERAN, AND THAT WE SHOULD REMAIN **OPTIMISTIC**, AS WE DID THEN.
ACTUALLY, THE MAHDI REVOLT'S A PERFECT EXAMPLE OF ENGLAND'S **COMPLACENCY**. WE WARRED ON A CULTURE WE DIDN'T UNDERSTAND...

...AND WE WERE MASSACRED.

MEN FROM
MARS

Hunngh. WHAT'S THE POINT OF ALL THIS, IF WE'RE NOT GOING NEAR THAT DAMN CRATER?
PRESUMABLY, WE ARE OBSERVING CONDITIONS HERE. THE HAMLET OF MAYBURY, FOR EXAMPLE, IS QUITE DESERTED...
WAIT A MINUTE. WHERE'S GRIFFIN?

I'D ASSUMED HE'D STAYED AT THE MUSEUM. HOLMES DIDN'T SPECIFY THAT WE SHOULD ALL ACCOMPANY THIS RECONNAISSANCE.
I--I SUPPOSE NOT.
THIS PISSING STORM'S GETTING WORSE. LET'S HOPE THAT LITTLE BASTARD'S HORSES DON'T--

What...?
ARRRR!

DRIVER, WHAT ARE YOU DOING? YOU ALMOST TURNED US OVER!
THAT LAST LIGHTNING FLASH. I THOUGHT I SAW SOMETHING!
WH-WHAT'S THAT NOISE, BENEATH THE THUNDER? IT'S ALMOST AS IF--

GOD'S BALLS.
BACK! GET BACK INSIDE THE COACH!
IT... IT'S LIKE A MILKING-STOOL...

JUST GET IN! WE HAVE TO GET WORD BACK TO LONDON!
COME ON, GIDDAP! YAAAA!

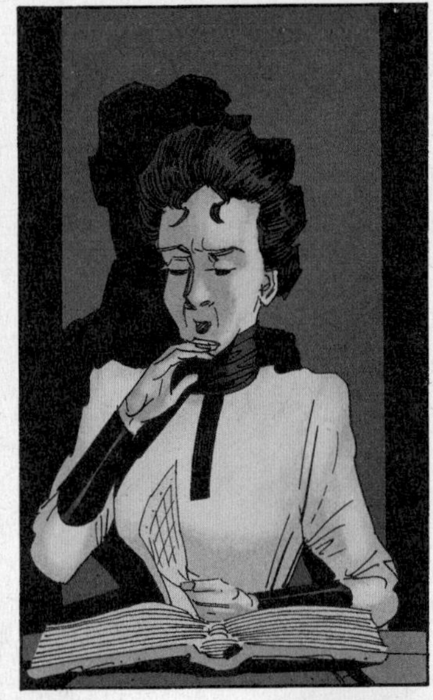

EYES ONLY
DOCTEUR OMEGA
UN HABITANT DE LA PLANÈTE MARS 1885

Mr. Griffin?

MR. GRIFFIN, WHAT ARE YOU DOING?
I-I KNOW YOU'RE HERE.
WHY... WHY AREN'T YOU SAYING ANYTHING?
GRIFFIN, I DEMAND TO KNOW WHAT'S--
...guu...
Oh!
OHHH!
NO. NO, DON'T...
PLEASE...
AAAA!
NO! LET GO OF--

Ouhhh...
Oh, God.

GOD...
LISTEN, PLEASE...
PLEASE DON'T...

AAAAA!

Aheheheh.

AAHUHH...
LOOK AT YOU, YOU STUCK-UP LITTLE TART.
WHAT ARE YOU? SAY IT!

I'M...
I-I'M A STUCK-UP LITTLE TART.
I'M A STUCK-UP LITTLE TART...

THAT'S RIGHT.
AA!

Aheh. NOW...
WHERE WAS I?

LEAGUE OF EXTRAORDINARY GENTLEMEN (America's Best Comics)

Whoa!
WHOAHH!

RIGHT. YOU LOT CLIMB OUT. I'LL CARRY ON OVER TO VAUXHALL AND REPORT TO M.
HE'LL PROBABLY WANT FETCHING BACK HERE TO THE MUSEUM.
NO DOUBT I'LL SEE YOU LATER.

GOD, WHAT A NIGHTMARE. THAT BLOODY MILKING STOOL THING...
WE'RE ALL IN THE MOST BEASTLY TROUBLE NOW. ALL OF US.
LET'S GET INSIDE, OUT OF THIS RAIN.

BUT YOU SAW HOW FAST IT MOVED, BOWLING ACROSS THE HORIZON.
A MACHINE LIKE THAT, IT MIGHT BE TOO MUCH EVEN FOR THE ARMY...
YOU REALIZE THERE MAY BE A SECOND SUCH DEVICE AT BYFLEET ?

OH, GOD. THAT SURREY GOLF LINKS, WHERE THE SECOND CYLINDER LANDED. I'D FORGOTTEN THAT.
TWO OF THEM. AND WE THOUGHT THEY COULDN'T LEAVE THE CRATER...
NO. THAT IS WHAT YOU ENGLISH ASSUMED. I THOUGHT OTHERWISE...

YES. YES, YOU SAID THEY'DE BE BUILDING SOME SORT OF VEHICLE.
WHILE WE WERE ALL HOPING FOR THE BEST, YOU WERE EXPECTING THE WORST.

It is as you stated. To hope for the best is an English failing.

Growing up in Mombai, in Calcutta, one learns differently...

YOU NEVER EVEN--
CRASH
SCOTT PILGRIM's
PRECIOUS LITTLE LIFE
VOL. 1
BRYAN LEE O'MALLEY
...

MR. PILGRIM! IT IS I, MATTHEW PATEL!
CONSIDER OUR FIGHT... BEGUN!!!

SCOTT PILGRIM (Oni Press)

GUYS, GET OFF THE STAGE.
PLUMTREE
the Archies
PLUMTREE
KPOK
KROWW
REVERSAL

SCOTT PILGRIM (Oni Press)

ALRIGHT... ALRIGHT...
MASS TEEN FAINTING
SCOTT!
HURK!!
SWOK
WHAT?
WATCH OUT! IT'S THAT ONE GUY!
OK, THANK YOU, WALLACE!

GRAPHIC NOVELS

SCOTT PILGRIM (Oni Press)

KRAK
HE'S GOING FOR THE AIR JUGGLE!
THIS GUY IS SUCH TOAST. DOESN'T HE KNOW THAT SCOTT'S THE BEST FIGHTER IN THE PROVINCE?
PLUMTREE

SCOTT PILGRIM (Oni Press)

POW
SOK
WHAP
SMURF
CHOP
SOCK
POM
64 HITS!!
45, 46...
THAT'S A NEW PERSONAL BEST, SCOTT!

SCOTT PILGRIM (Oni Press)

SO, PILGRIM, YOU'RE AS GOOD AS THEY SAY.
WHO THE HELL ARE YOU, ANYWAY?
the Androids
MASS TEEN FAINTING
MY NAME IS MATTHEW PATEL... AND I'M RAMONA'S FIRST EVIL EX-BOYFRIEND.

SCOTT PILGRIM (Oni Press)

CHOK
YOU'RE FIGHTING ME BECAUSE OF RAMONA?
YES! DIDN'T YOU GET MY E-MAIL AND LETTER EXPLAINING THE SITUATION?
PLUMTREE

I... SKIMMED THEM...?

I DELIVERED THAT LETTER PERSONALLY, IN THE MIDDLE OF A BLIZZARD! ***YOU'LL PAY!!***

WHAT'S WITH YOUR OUTFIT, ANYWAY? ARE YOU A PIRATE?

P...PIRATES ARE *IN* THIS YEAR!!

SO WHEN DID YOU DATE RAMONA?
I DON'T WANT TO TALK ABOUT IT!!
DODGE
C'MON, MAN, DISH! GOT ANY EMBARASSING STORIES?
Y... YOUR MOM IS AN EMBAR-ASSING STORY!
BLOCK
IT WAS IN THE SEVENTH GRADE.

SCOTT PILGRIM (Oni Press)

IT WAS FOOTBALL SEASON, AND THE LITTLE JOCKS WERE IN HIGH GEAR. FOR SOME REASON THEY ALL WANTED ME...

SCOTT PILGRIM (Oni Press)

MATTHEW PATEL WAS THE ONLY NON-WHITE, NON-JOCK KID IN SCHOOL. PROBABLY THE ONLY ONE FOR MILES AROUND, OR IN THE ENTIRE STATE, FOR ALL I KNOW. SO, OF COURSE...

KISSY KISSY

SCOTT PILGRIM (Oni Press)

WE JOINED FORCES AND TOOK 'EM ALL OUT. WE WERE ONE HELL OF A TEAM. NOTHING COULD BEAT MATTHEW'S MYSTICAL POWERS COMBINED WITH MY BRUTE STRENGTH.

NOTHING BUT PRE-ADOLESCENT CAPRICIOUSNESS.

SCOTT PILGRIM (Oni Press)

WE ONLY KISSED THE ONCE, AND WE WERE QUITS AFTER SOMETHING LIKE A WEEK AND A HALF.
HE DIDN'T GET REALLY EVIL UNTIL HIGH SCHOOL, AND BY THAT TIME HE'D MOVED FAR, FAR AWAY.
DUDE, WAIT... MYSTICAL POWERS?
Y-YOU'LL PAY FOR THIS, FLOWERS!!

SCOTT PILGRIM (Oni Press)

I BUILT YOU FIRST

Story: C.P. FREUND
Art: PETER and MARIA HOEY

YOU ARE WRECKED,
MY DEAR ROBOT
(HIS OLD FRIEND SAID),

AND YOUR SENSORY
DATA'S DISPERSED!

WHAT'S THE SHAPE OF THE WORLD
THAT YOU'VE BUILT
IN YOUR HEAD?

BAM

SHOT THE OTHER:

I BUILT YOU FIRST.

I BUILT YOU FIRST

BLAB 14

YOU'RE A PILE OF FALSE READINGS *(HIS OLD FRIEND FROWNED).*

YOUR RECEPTORS ALL SEEM TO BE CURSED!

YOU NO LONGER KNOW WHAT IS UP AND WHAT'S DOWN!

DROPPED THE OTHER:

I UPENDED YOU FIRST.

YOU'RE NOW ADDLED! CORRUPTED! COMPLETELY UNWOUND!
JUST OLD METAL REDUCED TO ITS WORST.
YOU'RE UNABLE TO KEEP EITHER FOOT ON THE GROUND!
SNAPPED THE OTHER:
I SUSPENDED YOU FIRST.

BLAB! (Fantagraphics)

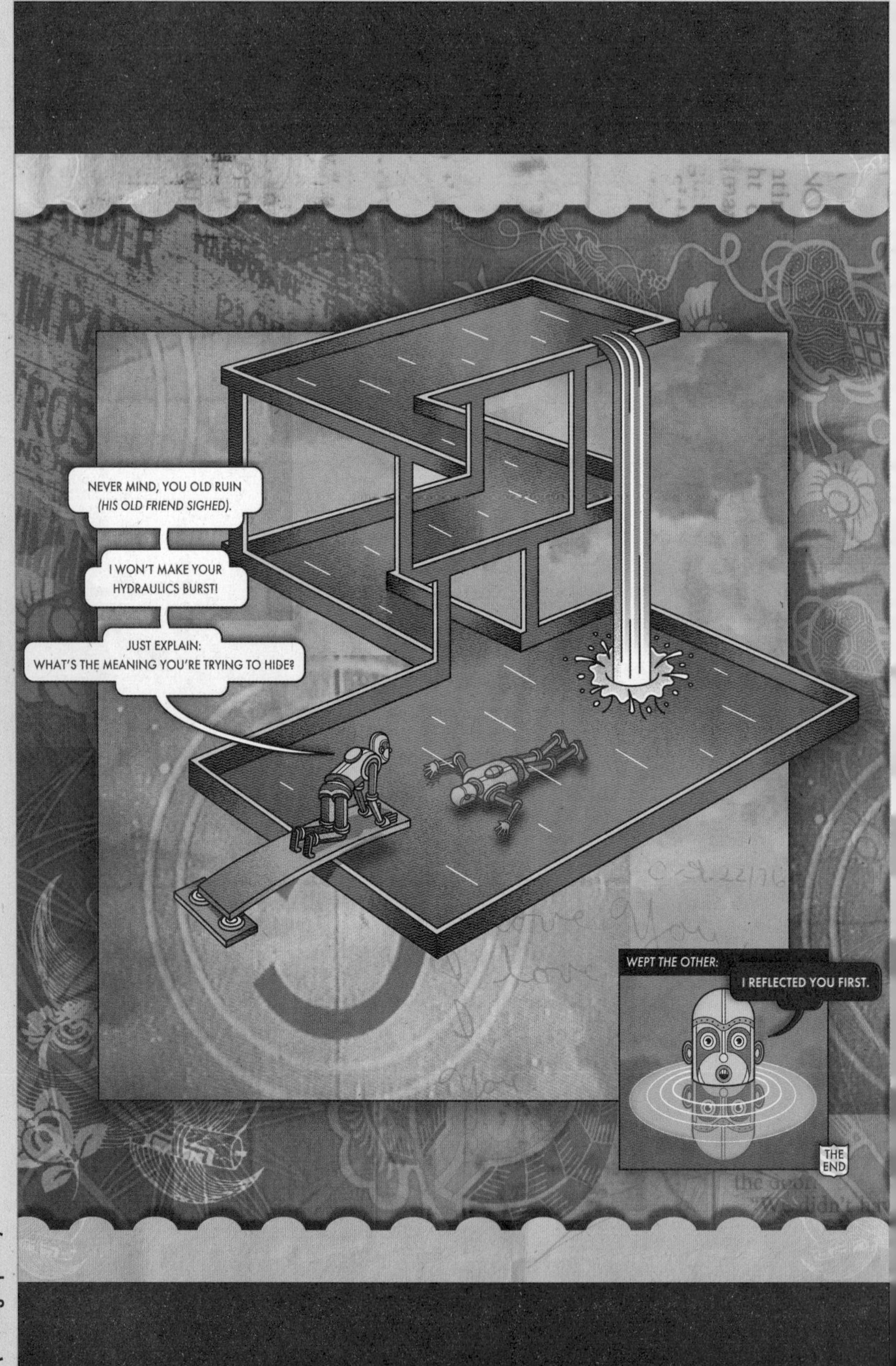
NEVER MIND, YOU OLD RUIN
(HIS OLD FRIEND SIGHED).
I WON'T MAKE YOUR
HYDRAULICS BURST!
JUST EXPLAIN:
WHAT'S THE MEANING YOU'RE TRYING TO HIDE?
WEPT THE OTHER:
I REFLECTED YOU FIRST.
THE END

A CHARLOTTE, N.C. LAWYER PURCHASED A BOX OF VERY RARE AND EXPENSIVE CIGARS...

...THEN INSURED THEM AGAINST FIRE, AMONG OTHER THINGS...

...WITHIN A MONTH, HAVING SMOKED HIS ENTIRE STOCKPILE OF THESE CIGARS...

...AND WITHOUT YET HAVING MADE EVEN HIS FIRST PREMIUM PAYMENT...

...THE LAWYER FILED CLAIM AGAINST THE INSURANCE COMPANY, SEEKING RECOMPENSE...

...FOR THE DESTRUCTION OF THE INSURED ITEMS IN A "SERIES OF SMALL FIRES'...

...THE INSURANCE COMPANY REFUSED TO PAY, CITING THE OBVIOUS REASON...

...THAT THE MAN HAD CONSUMED THE CIGARS IN THE NORMAL FASHION. THE LAWYER SUED, AND WON!

IN DELIVERING THE RULING THE JUDGE AGREED WITH THE INSURANCE COMPANY THAT THE CLAIM WAS FRIVOLOUS, BUT STATED NEVERTHELESS, THAT THE LAWYER HELD A POLICY IN WHICH THE COMPANY WARRANTED THAT THE CIGARS WERE INSURABLE AGAINST FIRE WITHOUT DEFINING WHAT IS CONSIDERED TO BE UNACCEPTABLE FIRE, AND THUS WAS OBLIGATED TO PAY THE CLAIM.

RATHER THAN ENDURE A LENGTHY, COSTLY APPEAL PROCESS...

...THE INSURANCE COMPANY PAID $15,000 TO THE LAWYER FOR HIS LOSS...

...AFTER THE LAWYER CASHED THE CHECK, THE COMPANY HAD HIM ARRESTED ON...

...24 COUNTS OF ARSON! THE LAWYER WAS CONVICTED OF INTENTIONALLY BURNING...

...PROPERTY AND SENTENCED TO 24 MONTHS IN JAIL AND A $24,000 FINE.

BLAB! (Fantagraphics)

COUPLA DAYS AGO.
SOMEWHERE OUT WEST.
1ST FED FIRST FEDERAL FARMERS
BANK
Andy's DINER
JUSTINE'S GOT THE GUNS.
LAST of the INDEPENDENTS
MATT FRACTION • KIERON DWYER
BILLY'S GOT THE WHEEL.
FIRE IT UP, BILLY.
I SEE YOU.

LAST OF THE INDEPENDENTS (AiT Planet Lar)

DUDE...
...WE'RE ROBBING THE BANK.

LAST OF THE INDEPENDENTS (AiT Planet Lar)

GOOD MORNING, SIR!
MA'AM. YOU HAVE MY MONEY.
I'D LIKE IT BACK.

IF I COULD JUST HAVE YOUR ACCOUNT NUMBER AND...
NO, MA'AM, I THINK YOU MISUNDERSTAND ME.
I WANT *ALL* THE MONEY.
STAY CALM AND ALL Y'ALL GO HOME WITH A GOOD STORY TO TELL.
AN' I'LL BE NEEDING TO SPEAK TO THE MANAGER.
ALARM, USE ONLY IN CASE OF EMERGENCY
(Robbery)→

Cool.
Yeah.
You. You You. You.
WANTED
RANCH ANAGER
MA'AM, IF YOU WOULDN'T MIND DROPPING YOUR GUNBELT TO THE FLOOR...
...AN' MR. MANAGER, I'M SURE YOU HIT THE ALARM ALREADY, SO WE'LL CUT TO THE CHASE.
The safe.
Now.
NO ONE'S GOING TO PLAY HERO HERE...
WHOOP-DEE-SHIT.
NOW IF YOU TWO COULD KINDLY...
OH NO.

LAST OF THE INDEPENDENTS (AiT Planet Lar)

SOMEBODY PUT A BUNCH OF MONEY IN OUR SAFE!
YOU PICKED THE WRONG BANK TO FUCK WITH, ASSHOLE.
DID YOU JUST CALL ME AN ASSHOLE?

AY LAKE TAY ATE, AY LAKE TAY ATE, AY LAKE TAY ATE ATE AYPLES AND BANAY-NAYS...
E LEEK TEE EAT, E LEEK TE EAT...
HERE COMES ACTION!
HERE COMES EXCITEMENT!
COLE! SIRENS!

LAST OF THE INDEPENDENTS (AiT Planet Lar)

LEAVE THE BAGS AND GET INSIDE THE SAFE NOW!
ACTIONACTIONACTION!
Be careful, Billy.
ACTION!
I ALWAYS TOLD STEVE HE SHOULD WEAR A SAFETY-BELT...
QUIET.
SOMETHING'S ABOUT TO HAPPEN.

LAST OF THE INDEPENDENTS (AiT Planet Lar)

THAT'S A VERY BIG MAN.

JESUS...
COPS ARE TAKEN CARE OF.
WE SAW, BILLY. BRING THE VAN AROUND...
...I'M GONNA NEED YOUR HELP WITH THE BAGS.
BAGS?

NO OBVIOUS SIGNS OF TRAUMA. HE APPEARS TO HAVE DIED IN HIS SLEEP.
YOU HAVE A CAUSE?
I'LL NEED AN AUTOPSY TO BE SURE, OF COURSE.
BUT IF I HAD TO GUESS, I'D SAY IT WAS A CEREBRAL HEMORRHAGE OF SOME SORT...OR PERHAPS AN ANEURYSM.
HIS RIGHT PUPIL IS EXPLODED, WHICH IS CONSISTENT WITH THAT FINDING.
IT'S A PITY. HE'S QUITE YOUNG.
HE'S TWENTY-SIX.
SIGH
TAP TAP TAP
WHEN WILL YOU MOVE HIM?
WHEN WE'RE DONE.
IT'S JUST THAT WE'RE BUSY THIS WEEK, THIS ROOM WAS SUPPOSED TO BE READY FOR--
WHEN WE'RE **DONE.**
BRITISH EMBASSY, PLEASE.
THANK YOU.
QUEEN & COUNTRY
OPERATION: STORM FRONT

QUEEN AND COUNTRY (Oni Press)

YES, THIS IS INSPECTOR ARAQUE WITH THE CARACAS METROPOLITAN POLICE...

...I'M CALLING TO REPORT THE DEATH OF A BRITISH NATIONAL.

...YES, I HAVE IT HERE.

EDWARD KITTERING.

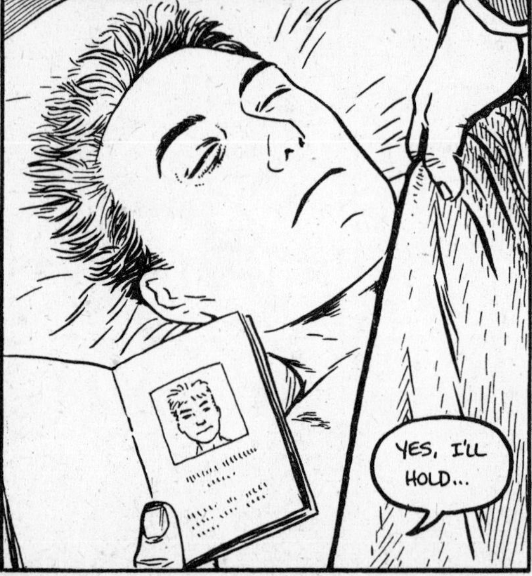

LONDON

"THE GOVERNMENT'S POLICY IS BOTH SHORT-SIGHTED AND ARROGANT COMMA AS RECENT EVENTS IN THE REGION HAVE PROVEN PERIOD.

READ THAT LAST BIT BACK.

"IF THIS CONTINUED DISREGARD IS MAINTAINED COMMA THE RESULTS WILL BE DISASTROUS COMMA NOT SOLELY ON A FINANCIAL COMMA BUT ALSO ON A HUMANITARIAN LEVEL."

FULL STOP.

TYPE IT UP FOR SIGNATURE, SEE IF WE CAN'T GET IT TO SIMON BY THE CLOSE OF PLAY. IF HE SIGNS OFF, HAVE SOMEONE RUN IT UP TO THE DEPUTY CHIEF AND THEN A COPY TO THE FOREIGN OFFICE.

YOU DON'T WANT TO SIT ON IT?

NO.

IT'S STRONG MEDICINE, PAUL. EVEN ***IF*** D. INT SIGNS OFF ON IT, YOU *KNOW* THAT THE DEPUTY CHIEF WILL POSITIVELY **BALK** AT CALLING THE PRIME MINISTER AND HIS CABINET ***FOOLS.***

I DIDN'T CALL THEM FOOLS. I CALLED THEM SHORT-SIGHTED AND ARROGANT.

JUST UNTIL TOMORROW--

PERHAPS YOU'D LIKE TO REWRITE IT **YOURSELF**, KATE?

I'LL TYPE IT UP.

WAIT A MOMENT.

THESE ARE FOR THE MINDERS.
AND I'M GETTING DAMN TIRED OF HAVING TO TRAFFIC EVERY PIECE OF PAPER THAT COMES THROUGH HERE.
YOU AND ME, BOTH.
JUST GET IT DONE.
AND WIPE THAT SMILE OFF YOUR FACE.
DREET
DREET
DREE
PLEASE, ALLOW ME.
P. A. TO D. OPS.
YES, HE'S HERE...
...I SEE.
...YES, HE'LL BE RIGHT DOWN.
YOU'RE WANTED IN THE OPS ROOM.

QUEEN AND COUNTRY (Oni Press)

THE PIT
THIS IS FUCKING KILLING ME.
SPECIAL OPERATIONS
WALLACE, T
HEAD OF SECTION
CHACE, T
KITTERING, E.
OH, FOR CHRIST'S SAKE, JUST DO IT ALREADY.
IS THAT SUPPOSED TO BE REVERSE PSYCHOLOGY?
NO, IT'S SUPPOSED TO BE ME WISHING YOU'D GIVE IT A BLOODY REST.
HERE, MY PACK, JUST HAVE A CIGARETTE AND SHUT UP ABOUT IT ALREADY.
I CAN'T, DAMMIT! I QUIT.
BMP
THEN STOP MOANING ABOUT IT AND BE QUIT ALREADY!
EASY TO SAY, HARDER TO DO. IT'S A PROCESS, AND YOU'RE NOT HELPING.
IT'S NOT A PROCESS ...
...IT'S A STATE.
SMOKING OR NON.
SCRIP!

EITHER YOU DO--
CHIK!
OR YOU DON'T.
I DO.
OH, YOU BASTARD...
YOU HEAR THAT, TARA? THEY'RE CALLING FOR YOU--
SIR?
BOSS? SLUMMING WITH THE WORKING CLASS ALL OF THE SUDDEN?
SHUT UP, TOM.
ED'S DEAD.

QUEEN AND COUNTRY (Oni Press)

CALL CAME FROM THE FCO OFFICE, VIA THE EMBASSY IN CARACAS.
HE WAS DISCOVERED THIS MORNING, IN HIS HOTEL ROOM, IN HIS BED.
THE CARACAS POLICE ARE INVESTIGATING.
DO THEY... I MEAN, DO WE...
ED WAS ONLY SUPPOSED TO BACK UP THE STATION ON THE LAUGHLIN SURVEILLANCE.
THAT'S ALL HE WAS DOING, RIGHT?
THAT'S ALL HE WAS DOING, TOM.
THE DUTY OPS OFFICER GOT A SIGNAL LAST NIGHT SAYING THEY'D WRAPPED UP, ED WAS SUPPOSED TO MAKE HIS WAY HOME TODAY.
CARACAS STATION CONFIRMS HE'D FINISHED. THEY'D FINISHED.
HOW?
WE DON'T KNOW. I'VE SENT THE CARACAS NUMBER TWO, JANICE O'HARE, OUT TO MAKE INQUIRIES.
RIGHT NOW, THE POLICE ARE SAYING IT LOOKS LIKE ED DIED IN HIS SLEEP.
THEY'LL DO AN AUTOPSY.
WE'LL KNOW MORE THEN.
BOLLOCKS.

QUEEN AND COUNTRY (Oni Press)

WHICH OF US GOES?
NEITHER OF YOU IS GOING ANYWHERE.
BOSS, THIS IS OUR MAN GOT MURDERED--
WE DON'T KNOW THAT. WE DON'T KNOW MUCH OF ANYTHING RIGHT NOW.
THE STATION IS HANDLING THE INVESTIGATION, AND ONCE THEY REPORT, I'LL MAKE A DECISION THEN.
JANICE O'HARE CAN'T FIND HER ASS WITH BOTH HANDS AND A ROAD MAP! YOU'VE GOT TO LET ONE OF US GO, PAUL!
IT'S TOO SOON. I'VE GOT TWO MINDERS, NOW, AND I'M NOT COMMITTING ONE OF THEM TO CARACAS IN THE HEAT OF GRIEF!
I NEED BOTH OF YOU WITH YOUR HEADS ON STRAIGHT.
E. KITTERING
ESPECIALLY YOU, TOM.
HAS ANYONE INFORMED HIS PARENTS?
THEY'RE DIVORCED. HIS MOTHER STILL LIVES IN BOURNEMOUTH. BUT HIS FATHER'S IN DOVER.
NOT YET.
I'LL DO IT.

QUEEN AND COUNTRY (Oni Press)

I WAS HIS HEAD OF SECTION. I SHOULD DO IT.
ALL RIGHT, BUT NOT YET.
NOT UNTIL WE KNOW WHEN WE'RE GETTING THE BODY BACK.

FIRST THING TOMORROW, I WANT YOU TO HEAD OUT TO THE SCHOOL, SEE IF THERE'S A REPLACEMENT FOR ED IN TRAINING.
WE'RE PLUCKING A VIRGIN?

NO CHOICE.
THERE'S NO ONE IN ROSTER SLATED FOR SPECIAL OPERATIONS.
IS THERE ANYTHING I CAN DO?

YOU CAN CLEAR OUT ED'S DESK.
E. KITTERIN

I'VE GOT TO INFORM C AND THE DEPUTY CHIEF.

QUEEN AND COUNTRY (Oni Press)

HOW ARE YOU **DOING**?

HOW DO YOU **THINK**?

E. KITTERING

I COULD ASK **YOU** THE SAME.

I'M DOING POORLY.

AND **I** NEVER SLEPT WITH HIM.

WE HADN'T REALLY TALKED SINCE IT ENDED, YOU KNOW?

NOT OUTSIDE OF THE OFFICE, AT LEAST. NOT ABOUT ANYTHING THAT WASN'T **WORK**.

IF HE *WAS* MURDERED, **I** WANT THE JOB. I WANT TO SETTLE IT. I OWE ED THAT.

NO MORE THAN **I** DO.

AS YOU JUST POINTED OUT, **YOU** WEREN'T SLEEPING WITH HIM.

I WOULDN'T TRY THAT ARGUMENT ON CROCKER.
YOU'LL NEED SOME BOXES.

...I'LL GO GET THEM

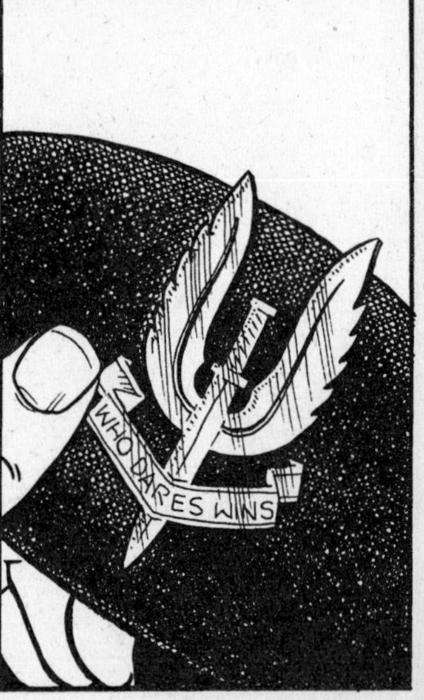
WHO DARES WINS

"THE LINE'S" TRAIN STATION WAS A LOYAL REFLECTION OF ITS NEIGHBORHOOD. AN IMAGE OF WHAT IT COULD HAVE BEEN BUT NEVER WAS. TEN YEARS AGO, THE CONSTRUCTION OF THE SITE HAD STOPPED, LEAVING IT HALF BUILT. ALONG WITH THE FACTORIES CLOSED BECAUSE OF THE CRISIS, IT TOOK PART IN THE GHOSTLY SCENERY OF THIS SUBURB.
WEEKLY HAD DISAPPEARED, AND DON'T ASK ME WHY, BUT DESPITE IT ALL, I KIND OF MISSED HIS "FINE SMELL."
SO I DECIDED TO FOLLOW THE MAGPIE, WHO I THOUGHT WAS A LOT LESS INNOCENT THAN HE APPEARED TO BE.

HOW MUCH WILL YOU GIVE ME FOR THIS ?

WHERE'S THE OWNER OF THAT CAMERA?

I DON'T KNOW WHAT YOU'RE TALKING ABOUT, MISTER...
I'M TALKING ABOUT MY FRIEND, THE REPORTER. I'M AFRAID HE'S BEEN KIDNAPPED AND YOU MIGHT KNOW WHERE HE IS.

BLACKSAD (ibooks, inc.)

I DON'T KNOW ANYTHING. THEY NEVER TELL ME ANYTHING.
THEY?

AND WHAT'S YOUR ROLE IN ALL THIS? YOU'VE BEEN FOLLOWING ME SINCE THE DAY I STEPPED FOOT IN THIS STINKING PLACE. YOU'RE A DAMN BIRD OF ILL OMEN.

I'M JUST A POOR DEVIL WHO ONLY WANTS TO LIVE LONG ENOUGH TO GET TO GO TO LAS VEGAS...

YOU LIKE TO GAMBLE, HUH? OK, OLD MAN, LET'S PLAY A LITTLE GAME: I ASK QUESTIONS AND YOU ANSWER!

WHERE ARE "THEY" HIDING MY FRIEND? ANSWER ME!

OK! I'LL TAKE YOU TO HIM! JUST DON'T KILL ME, I BEG YOU!

LET'S GO. TIME IS RUNNING OUT.

BLACKSAD (ibooks, inc.)

TELL ME THAT THERE'S NOTHING BETWEEN YOU AND HUK.

I'M SURPRISED YOU EVEN PAID ATTENTION TO THAT JERK. YOU KNOW BETTER THAN ANYONE THAT I'D NEVER LET ANY MAN TOUCH ME. IT DISGUSTS ME WAY TOO MUCH!

GOD, JEZZ! IT'S UNBEARABLE TO THINK THAT SOMEONE ELSE IS ENJOYING WHAT I'VE BEEN DENIED FOR SO LONG...

OH, CALM DOWN HANS! YOU KNEW EXACTLY WHAT WAS IN STORE FOR YOU WHEN WE ARRANGED OUR MARRIAGE. ANYWAY, IT LOOKS LIKE YOU'VE FOUND SOMEONE TO CONSOLE YOU, HAVEN'T YOU?

I MEAN, THOSE CHOIR KIDS TO WHOM YOU ARE SO DEVOTED...

...OH!

DON'T YOU DARE EVER REPEAT WHAT YOU'VE JUST SAID! YOU KNOW THAT'S AN INFAMOUS LIE!

WHAT WOULD YOU DO? MAKE A SCENE BY THROWING ME OUT OF THE HOUSE, LIKE YOU DID WITH YOUR FIRST WIFE? NO, UNFORTUNATELY FOR YOU, I'M NOT SOME POOR BLACK GIRL LIKE SHE WAS.

BLACKSAD (ibooks, inc.)

AND YOU NEED ME TO KEEP YOUR IMAGE OF THE PERFECT WASP, HONEST MAN AND GOOD HUSBAND. DON'T YOU REMEMBER? THAT'S WHY WE GOT MARRIED.

DAMN YOU! GET OUT OF MY SIGHT!

WITH PLEASURE!

SLAM!

BISHOP, BRING THE ROPES THAT ARE IN THE TRUNK.

I KNOW THIS PLACE LIKE THE PALM OF MY HAND. I USED TO WORK HERE WHEN IT WAS THE BIGGEST PLANE FACTORY IN THE COUNTRY. I COULD MOVE THROUGH IT WITH MY EYES CLOSED! HA-HA!
OLDSMILL AIRCRAFT INDUSTRIES
NO TRESPASSING

IT WAS THE ONLY THING I COULD DO TO SERVE MY COUNTRY. I COULDN'T JOIN IN COMBAT BECAUSE OF MY BEING BLIND AND ALL.

AND I WOULD HAVE PREFERRED TO NEVER TO HAVE SEEN WHAT I SAW OVER THERE.

WHERE WERE YOU POSTED? IN EUROPE? I WOULD'VE LIKED TO BE A PILOT.

IRONIC ISN'T IT ? A BIRD WHO CAN'T FLY.

TROMP!

IT'S NOT THE FIRST TIME THAT A VERMIN LIKE YOU LEAD ME TO A TRAP, YOU KNOW, COTTEN...

...COTTEN?

WE WERE WAITING FOR YOU.
LET'S BEGIN THEN.
OF COURSE...
BOYS... GO AHEAD!
HEYYY!
HAVE YOU ALL GONE MAD? LET GO OF ME! I SAID LET GO OF ME!

BLACKSAD (ibooks, inc.)

WHAT?

WHAT A YOU MEAN,

GET UP?

DOGS AND WATER (Drawn and Quarterly)

DOGS AND WATER (Drawn and Quarterly)

OH MAN, YOU'RE ALL SMASHED UP
OW
GH
ACHEM
YAWN
CRACK
OW.
WHAT SHOULD WE DO? WE CAN'T JUST LEAVE HIM HERE RIGHT? HE'S STILL ALIVE.
OF COURSE. HE DID TRY TO KILL ME.

DOGS AND WATER (Drawn and Quarterly)

I COULD TRY TO CARRY HIM... BUT I DON'T THINK WE'D GET VERY FAR.
ESPECIALLY WITH MY NECK LIKE THIS.
DO YOU WANT SOME OF THIS REINDEER MEAT?
WHAT?
CKG
WATER.
YOU WANT SOME WATER.
YOU'RE NOT GOING TO CHOKE ME AGAIN ARE YOU?
HHUH-UH

IS THAT ALRIGHT
YEAH.
THANKS
WHAT HAPPENED
WE WERE JUST GETTING INTO THE HELICOPTER TO LEAVE...
THE NEXT THING I REMEMBER IS WAKING UP HERE ON THE GROUND
AND YOU CAN'T MOVE?
NO.
BUT YOU DID MOVE... YOU...WRESTLED ME TO THE GROUND... YOU ALMOST KILLED ME.
YEAH... I DON'T...
I THOUGHT YOU WERE ONE OF THEM.
?
WHAT ARE YOU DOING OUT HERE?
I'M
I'M... JUST PASSING THROUGH...

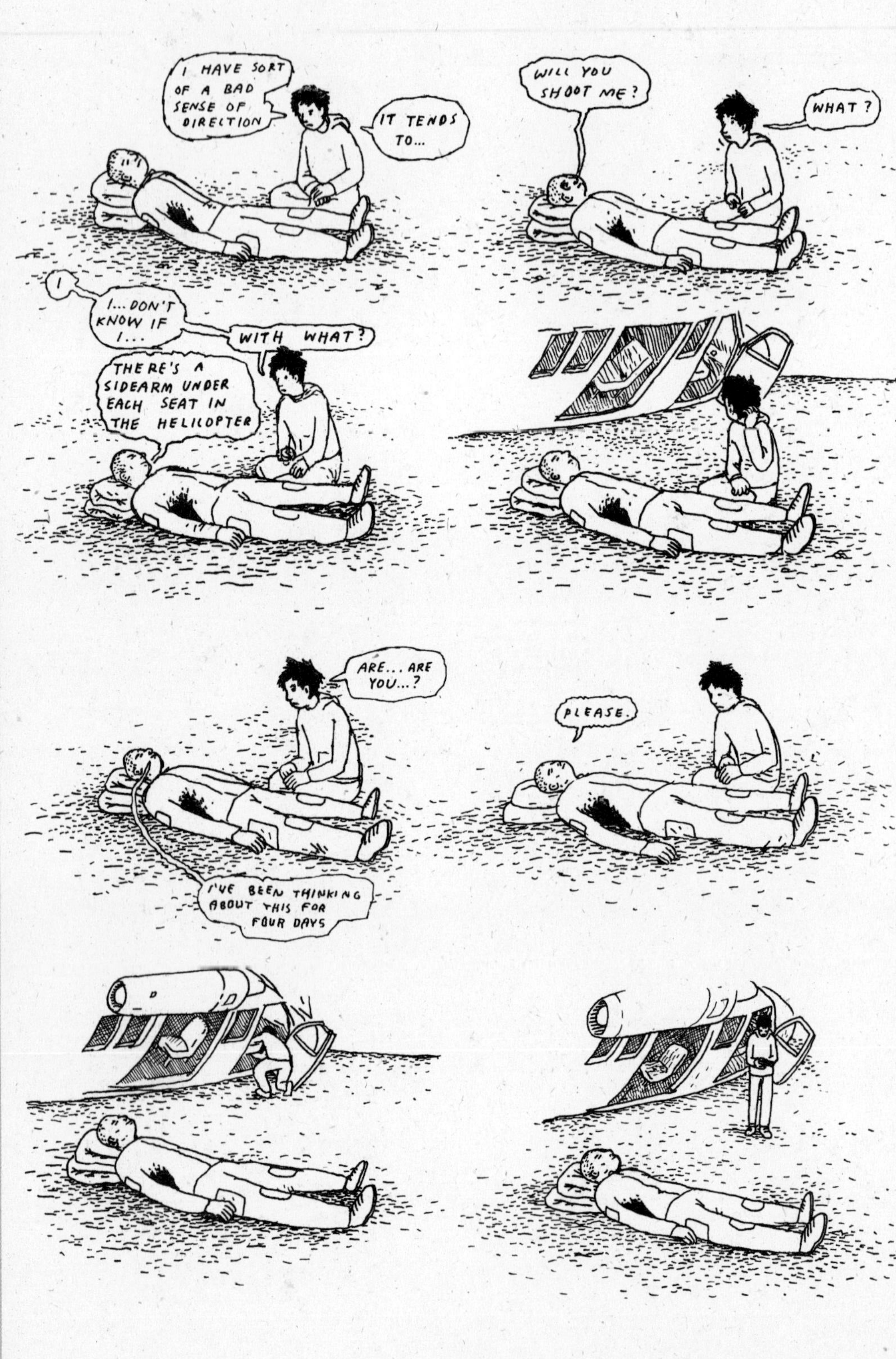
I HAVE SORT OF A BAD SENSE OF DIRECTION
IT TENDS TO...
WILL YOU SHOOT ME?
WHAT?
I
I... DON'T KNOW IF I...
WITH WHAT?
THERE'S A SIDEARM UNDER EACH SEAT IN THE HELICOPTER
ARE... ARE YOU...?
I'VE BEEN THINKING ABOUT THIS FOR FOUR DAYS
PLEASE.

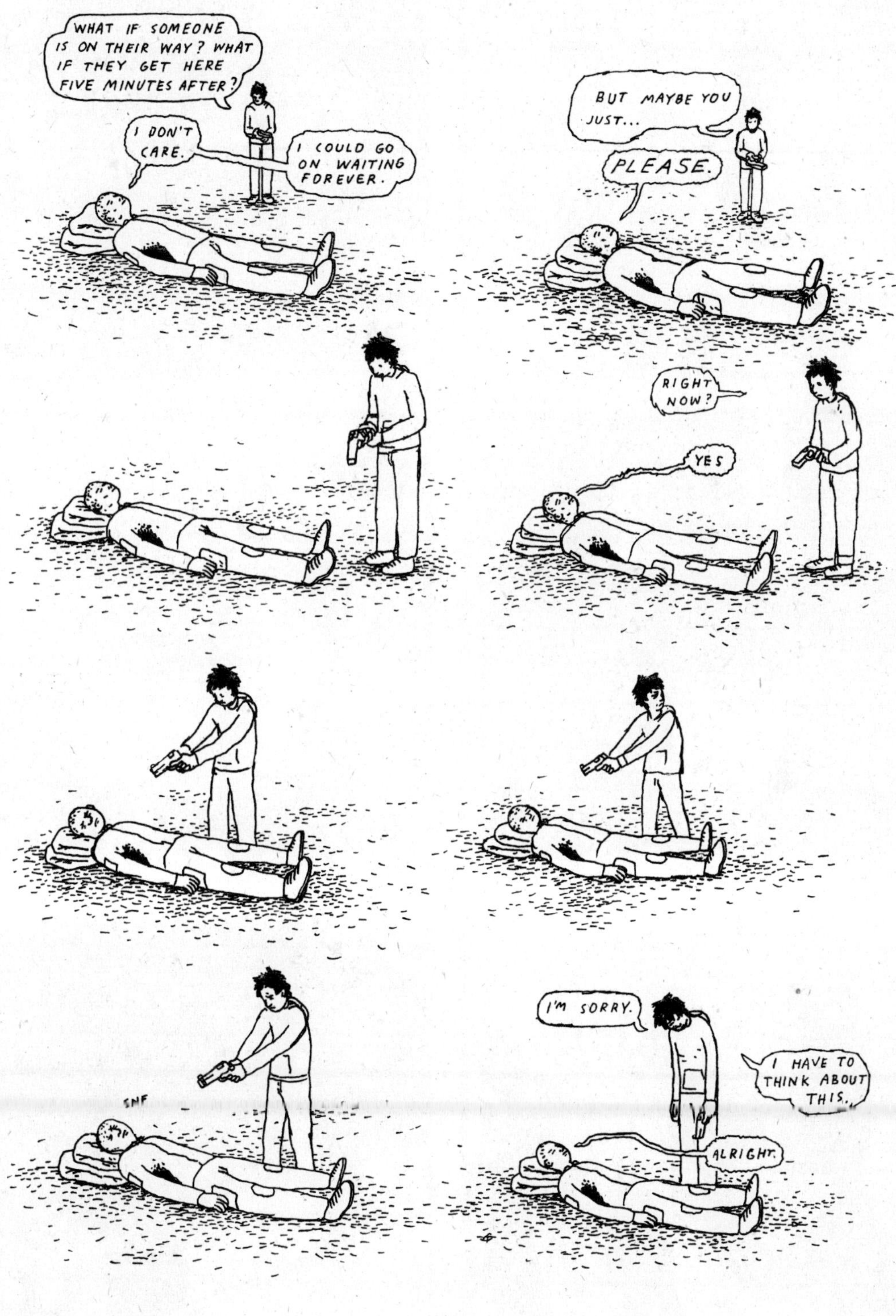
WHAT IF SOMEONE IS ON THEIR WAY? WHAT IF THEY GET HERE FIVE MINUTES AFTER?
I DON'T CARE.
I COULD GO ON WAITING FOREVER.
BUT MAYBE YOU JUST...
PLEASE.
RIGHT NOW?
YES
SNF
I'M SORRY.
I HAVE TO THINK ABOUT THIS.
ALRIGHT.

YOU CAN'T GET THERE FROM HERE (Fantagraphics)

YOU CAN'T GET THERE FROM HERE (Fantagraphics)

THE WAR IN EUROPE DIDN'T SLOW NUCLEAR PHYSICS RESEARCH APPRECIABLY —ESPECIALLY SINCE SO MANY TOP PHYSICISTS HAD HEADED *WEST.* **OTTO FRISCH** AND **RUDOLPH PEIERLS*** HAD SETTLED IN *ENGLAND* WHILE OTHERS, LIKE **FERMI** AND **EINSTEIN** BEFORE THEM, ENDED UP IN THE *U.S.*

BUT THE WAR **DID** LEND SOME *URGENCY* TO THAT RESEARCH, EVEN THOUGH THE PREDOMINANT VIEW WAS STILL MUCH LIKE **RUTHERFORD'S** IN 1933:

?
ONE TIMELY WORD OF WARNING IS ISSUED TO THOSE WHO LOOK FOR SOURCES OF POWER IN ATOMIC TRANSMUTATIONS— —SUCH EXPECTATIONS ARE THE MEREST *MOONSHINE*.

BOHR *SHARED* THIS VIEW, THOUGH FOR *ENGINEERING* RATHER THAN SCIENTIFIC/THEORETICAL REASONS.

LISTEN, **TELLER**. THE AMERICANS ESTIMATE THAT IT WILL TAKE THEM 10 DAYS OF AROUND-THE-CLOCK OPERATION TO SEPARATE ONE THOUSAND MILLIONTH OF A *GRAM* OF **U-235** FROM RAW URANIUM ORE.
U.S. MAP
WHY, YOU'D HAVE TO TURN THE *WHOLE COUNTRY* INTO A **FACTORY** TO MAKE ANY PROGRESS AT ALL!

ABOUT A MONTH AFTER **FRISCH** AND **PEIERLS** MADE PUBLIC THEIR CALCULATIONS ON THE CRITICAL MASS OF ***U-235*** NEEDED FOR A *BOMB*— IT WAS ***NOT* TONS**, BUT IT *WAS* A LOT MORE THAN ONE THOUSAND MILLIONTH OF A GRAM! — *GERMANY* OCCUPIED *DENMARK* TO ENSURE THAT THE COUNTRY WOULD "ACCEPT THE PROTECTION OF THE REICH."

* RUDOLPH E. PEIERLS WAS (YET ANOTHER) OF *BOHR'S* COLLABORATORS. A TOP-NOTCH MATHEMATICIAN, A REFUGEE ... AND THE AUTHOR OF "*THE ATOM THAT BOHR BUILT.*"

BOHR HAD JUST COME FROM *NORWAY*, WHERE HE HAD REPORTED ON THE CONFIRMATION OF HIS **U-235** THEORY.

UPON HIS RETURN TO *COPENHAGEN*, HE WAS EFFECTIVELY UNDER HOUSE ARREST.

MESSAGES URGING **BOHR** TO *LEAVE IMMEDIATELY* BEGAN TO ARRIVE AT THE INSTITUTE. WITH A JEWISH MOTHER AND THEIR WORK ON PLACING **REFUGEE** INTELLECTUALS WELL KNOWN, **NIELS**, **HARALD** AND THEIR FAMILIES WERE TARGETS.

BUT THEY DECIDED TO STAY, SINCE THE **BOHR** BROTHERS WERE ALSO **SYMBOLS OF** *DANISH CULTURE* IN THE FACE OF **NAZI** EFFORTS TO ESTABLISH DOMINANCE. NOT SO MUCH BY PHYSICAL MEANS (YET), BUT MORE SUBTLY.

THEY ESTABLISHED A *GERMAN CULTURAL INSTITUTE* RIGHT AWAY, AND IN 1941 **HEISENBERG** GAVE A PUBLIC LECTURE THERE. **BOHR** CHOSE NOT TO ATTEND, BUT...
HERR DOKTOR PROFESSOR HEISENBERG — HERE FOR BOHR.
MY PAPERS...
ALL IS IN ORDER, HERR DOKTOR PROFESSOR. HE'S INSIDE.

WERNER.
WHY HAVE YOU COME?

PROFESSOR, SO GOOD OF YOU TO HAVE ME.

"HAVE YOU." I NEED **HARDLY** STRESS THAT ...
BUT WHY HAVE YOU COME?

I NEED ...
I WANT ...

TO TALK. JUST TO TALK. PHYSICS.

THERE ARE THINGS I ... WE SHOULD DISCUSS.

PERHAPS THERE ARE.

AND SO THEY TALKED, JUST AS THEY HAD IN THE PAST. AND... *NOT* JUST LIKE IN THE PAST, FOR **HEISENBERG** HAD STAYED IN *GERMANY* AND IN DOING SO HAD — IN THE MINDS OF MANY — TACITLY ENDORSED THE NAZIS.

HE SAW IT DIFFERENTLY, OF COURSE.

THE NATIONAL SOCIALISTS DON'T HONOR SCIENCE, SO OF COURSE THEY TREAT SCIENTISTS BADLY.
BUT WHEN THIS IS OVER THEIR ATTITUDE WILL CHANGE.
AS I TOLD FERMI, I FEEL... RESPONSIBLE TO THE YOUNGER GENERATION OF GERMAN PHYSICISTS.
SOMEONE MUST HELP THEM CARRY ON THE TRADITION OF SCIENCE, EVEN DURING... THIS.
AS YOU WERE TO ME, I MUST BE TO THEM.

PROFESSOR, COULD WE WALK THROUGH THE WOODS AS WE USED TO?
WE HAD SO MANY OF OUR BEST CONVERSATIONS THERE.
IF IT IS PERMITTED.
IT WAS. SO THEY WALKED.

WHY HAVE WE COME HERE?
WHY HAVE *YOU* COME HERE?

SURELY YOU KNOW OF **GERMANY'S**... *REQUISITIONS* FROM THE **NORSK HYDRO PLANT.**
SO... WELL...

WE ARE USING *HEAVY WATER* TO...
HEISENBERG.

WERNER. *WHATEVER* IT IS...
DID **HEISENBERG** HAVE A *DRAWING*?

GRAPHIC NOVELS

SUSPENDED IN LANGUAGE (GT Labs)

DID HE HAVE CALCULATIONS?
IF YOU HAVE CALCULATIONS—WELL, YOU KNOW THAT'S NOT HOW I...
AND I WOULD BE ASHAMED TO KNOW THAT IT'S HOW YOU WOULD APPROACH...

DID HE HAVE A MESSAGE FOR BOHR?
IF IT'S A LETTER TO ME, TELL ME WHAT IT SAYS. HERE. NOW. WE WILL DISCUSS THINGS.

BUT IF YOU WANT ME TO PASS ALONG SOMETHING TO OTHERS, I...
I NEED HARDLY STRESS THAT I CAN'T BE A MESSENGER, FOR YOU, UNDER THESE CIRCUMSTANCES.

WAS THERE EVEN A PIECE OF PAPER AT ALL? WHAT HAPPENED IS UN-CLEAR TO THIS DAY, SINCE NEITHER SPOKE OF THEIR MEETING IN DETAIL TO ANYONE.

AND THEY WERE ALONE IN THE WOODS.

205

I AM THE QUEEN OF DARA DESS.
THE REMAINS
I AM THE QUEEN OF A BROKEN CITADEL TWO HUNDRED AND FIFTY MILES AWAY ACROSS HILL AND DALE AND CRAG.
I HAVE SAID SO, AND MEN AND WOMEN HAVE BELIEVED ME.
LET THEM KNOW WE'RE HERE.
LET LOOSE!
INDEED, I THINK SOME BELIEVED I WAS A QUEEN BEFORE I DID.
31
ARTESIA

ARTESIA (Archaia Studio Press)

AND NOW THAT I HAVE CLAIMED MY THRONE, I MUST BEGIN MY DEFENSE OF IT UNDER WATCHFUL EYES.
NOT JUST OF THOSE THAT WOULD CONDEMN ME FOR MY CLAIM...
...OR WHO WOULD TAKE IT FROM ME FOR THEIR OWN...
...BUT OF THE GHOSTS IN MY HEAD, WHO SAW MY HESITATION ON THE BRINK OF QUEENSHIP, AND NAMED IT GUILT OR FEAR OR DOUBT.
WHO WATCH ME NOW IN UNENDING VIGILANCE, AND WHISPER TO ME MY SECRETS, MY PASTS, MY OTHER SELVES...
...BECAUSE THEY ARE ME, AND I AM THEM.
OPEN YOUR EYES. SEE THE WORLD. OPEN YOUR EARS. HEAR THE WORLD.
SEE YOUR ENEMIES. HEAR THEIR PRAYERS.

I PRICK UP MY EARS, AND LISTEN TO THE SPIRITS AT PLAY ON THE WINDS.
THEY BRING ME THE BABBLE OF AN EMPIRE...

...TONGUES AND DIALECTS APLENTY.
BUT MY MOTHER'S ART CAN MAKE THEM CLEAR.

‹ VANI! HEAR ME! GIVE ME YOUR EAGLE'S STRENGTH! ›
‹ GENICHÉ! SEND YOUR HERALDS FOR ME! ›
‹ I CALL UPON MY ANCESTORS! ›
‹ MÉDÜRE! GUIDE OUR SWORDS! ›
VICTORIA!
THEY CALL UPON THE OLD GODS. *OUR* GODS.
AND SOME NOT SO OLD. AND SOME NOT OURS.
BUT *NOT* THE DIVINE KING.

AYE. AND THEY'RE TRYING TO BREAK OUT....
OVER THERE.
RIGHT.
LET'S TAKE A LOOK!
THE WIND BRINGS THE THRUM OF BOWSTRINGS, THE HISS OF ARROW SHAFTS...
KEEP THE COMPANIES TO THEIR ARROWS...
...AND TRUST OUR ALLIES WILL HOLD THE LINE!
....HOOVES ON THE EARTH....
...THE RING OF STEEL ON STEEL.
VICTORIA!

YOU SHOULDN'T RISK YOURSELF IN SO MINOR AN ACTION, YOUR GRACE!
I KNOW, HARCAS...
BUT I STILL *WANT* TO.
RETRISE! RETRISE!

RIGHT! CHECK THE LINE! GET ME A ROLL CALL!
BARON! THE DARADJ QUEEN IS HERE.

BARON WALLIS.
YOUR GRACE! I HOPE WE DID NOT TROUBLE YOU...
THAT WAS A STRONG COMPANY TRYING TO FIGHT ITS WAY OUT....
...BUT THEY MADE THE MISTAKE OF PICKING OUR PART OF THE LINE.

THESE ARE MY LANDS, AFTER ALL...
...AND THOUGH I AM OFTEN ON CAMPAIGN WITH THE GRAND DUKE...
...I DO NOT SUFFER INVADERS LIGHTLY.

A VASSAL OF YOURS HOLDS THIS BRIDGE?
AYE, IT IS IN THE KEEPING OF MY UNCLE, LORD GARIN.
BUT HE RODE WITH US TO COLLWYN...
NEPHEW! YOUR GRACE!
MY SON OSGAR WAS TO HOLD THIS BRIDGE IN MY ABSENCE...
HE WILL, AS LONG AS HE IS ABLE.
WE HAVE A STRONG TOWER, BUT AGAINST THREE THOUSAND THESSIDS....
IT'LL SOON FALL.
THEN WE ARRIVED JUST IN TIME.
YHERA'S FORTUNE THAT THE THESSIDS ARE STILL REELING FROM OUR VICTORY...
...AND THAT WE CAPTURED THEIR SIEGE ENGINEERS AT THE BATTLE OF COLLWYN.
MAKE WAY!
THE FATES SMILE UPON US.
OSGAR WILL SOON BE SAFE, UNCLE.
OUR BROTHER HAS ALWAYS HAD THE SPRING QUEEN'S LUCK, YOUR GRACE!
BORN UNDER THE MIDNIGHT STAR, HE WAS.
WE THOUGHT WE'D HAVE A STORY TO TELL HIM...

...BUT NOW HE CAN BOAST HE HELD OFF *THREE THOUSAND* THESSIDS FOR TWO DAYS!
KING CASLAV!
WE'LL NEED HIS LUCK IN THE MORNING, YOUNG LIEFRING.

IT WAS AS YOU SUSPECTED, ARTESIA.
WE ARE ONLY THREE THOUSAND OURSELVES.
KING COLIN KEPT MARCHING ON WITH HIS VASSALS.
I SENT MY HERALDS, BUT HE'S INTENT ON HEADING EAST UNTIL HE FINDS THE HIGH KING.

HE WANTS NO MORE TO DO WITH US.
WITH ***YOU***, I'M AFRAID.
AND OUR REARGUARD IS STRUNG BETWEEN HERE AND COLLWYN....
...AND WON'T BE HERE FOR DAYS YET.

BUT WE HAVE THE HIGH GROUND...
...AND ARE FRESH WITH VICTORY!
ONE THING TO DEFEND AT THESE ODDS OR WORSE...
...BUT THE NUMBERS ARE TOO EVEN TO RISK AN ATTACK.
A MAN I KILLED ONCE TOLD ME THE BEST BATTLE IS ONE YOU DON'T HAVE TO FIGHT TO WIN.
I DO NOT BELIEVE IT, MYSELF.
BUT THE TIME MAY HAVE COME TO PUT THAT SAYING TO THE TEST.
LET US SEE WHAT THE MORNING STAR BRINGS US, YES?
I AM SURPRISED WHEN THEY AGREE. THE MIDDLE KINGDOMS SELDOM SEE QUEENS WHO ACT AS CAPTAINS...
...LET ALONE A CAPTAIN PLAYING AT A THRONE.
DID YOUR HEAR WALLIS' COUSINS TALK OF THE SPRING QUEEN?
THEY MAY FOLLOW THE DIVINE KING, BUT EVEN THE AURIANS STILL REMEMBER AN-ATHAIR.
AYE, BUT NOT ALL OF THEM. KING COLIN AND THE DAINPHALIANS WILL BE A PROBLEM...

ARTESIA (Archaia Studio Press)

THOUGH PERHAPS NOT BY THEIR *ABSENCE*.
WE HAVE HAD A CHANCE TO TAKE THE MEASURE OF OUR ALLIES.
THE FORCES WE HAVE WITH US WILL STAND WELL IN BATTLE TOMORROW.
BUT THE THESSIDS...

AYE. THE *THESSIDS*.
THE THESSIDS SCARE ME.
THIS CAMPAIGN IS TOO WELL PLANNED, AND THERE ARE TOO MANY OF THEM.
AND WE HAVEN'T EVEN SEEN THEIR MAIN HOST YET.

THE *ISLIKLIDS* SCARE ME.
THE ISLIKLID SCARES ME.
I CAN'T BELIEVE THERE'S ONLY ONE OF THEM LURKING IN THEIR HOST...
...OR WHAT IT DID TO OUR CAMP.

THEN THERE ARE THE PRISONERS TO CONSIDER.
BETWEEN OUR VARIOUS CAMPS, WE'VE CLOSE TO ***TWO THOUSAND*** OF THEM.
WE CAN'T FEED THEM ALL.
...AND IF THEY RECOVER THEIR WITS, AND SEE HOW ***FEW*** HOLD THEM...

TWO THOUSAND THESSID PRISONERS BEHIND US.
THREE THOUSAND THESSIDS IN FRONT OF US.
MAY THE MORNING STAR BRING US A WAY TO BE RID OF ***BOTH***.

ARTESIA (Archaia Studio Press)

I DON'T KNOW WHY THE REBBE'S DEATH STRUCK ME SO HARD. DEATH AND DYING WERE ALL AROUND ME EVERY WAKING HOUR OF THE DAY. ON THE STREETS LAY THE BODIES OF THOSE WHO COULD NO LONGER STAND. IGNORED, THEY WAITED PATIENTLY, QUIETLY, FOR THE CREAKING CART TO COME BY AND PICK THEM UP. THEN, TO BE THROWN ON LIKE A SACK OF LOOSE BONES, PILED ONTO THE CHALKY BODIES BENEATH.

BUT, THE REBBE HAD SURVIVED THE FIRE. ESCAPED THE CAMP. ELUDED PUNISHMENT AND DEATH TO SNEAK INTO THE GHETTO. TO BE ABSORBED INTO THE ONLY PLACE HE FELT SAFE. WITH HIS PEOPLE.

OH, THE IRONY. THE SADNESS OF IT ALL.

"HIS DEATH MUST BE MARKED, MORDECAI. IT MUST NOT GO UNNOTICED."

"HOW DO YOU PROPOSE THAT SHOULD BE DONE, YOSSEL?"

Joe Kubert

yossel

THE NEXT MORNING, I APPROACHED THE GREY WALLS OF THE SECURITY POLICE BUILDING. THE SKY WAS SMUDGED WITH BLACK SMOKE RISING FROM BUILDINGS ALREADY REDUCED TO RUBBLE AND BURNING.
OUR CAPTORS WERE HERDING THE GHETTO'S REMNANT OCCUPANTS INTO TIGHTER GROUPS BY REDUCING THE HABITABLE AREAS WITH RELENTLESS PRECISION.

YOSSEL (ibooks inc.)

I PLACED MY CAP UNDER MY CHAIR.
NOTHING EXISTED FOR ME EXCEPT MY DRAWINGS THAT SEEMED TO FLOW FROM MY PENCIL. I FELT A NUMBNESS, A PRESSURE JUST ABOVE AND BEHIND MY EYES.
HOW THEY LAUGHED AND JOKED AT THE PICTURES I DREW. THEY WERE AMUSED BY THE MUSCULAR HEROES. "TRUE NAZIS", THEY SAID. "RULERS OF THE WORLD."
"LOOK HOW THE LITTLE JEW DRAWS."
"THE PENCIL- IT MOVES SO FAST."
"IT IS A GIFT. HE IS SO LUCKY."
I DID NOT LOOK BACK AS I WALKED AWAY FROM THE BUILDING. FROM MY AUDIENCE OF SMILING, JOKING ADMIRERS. THEIR LAUGHTER FADED WITH EVERY STEP I TOOK AWAY FROM THAT HATED PLACE.

YOSSEL (ibooks inc.)

THEN THE EXPLOSION ERUPTED. IT WAS DEAFENING. I FELT THE BLAST ACROSS MY BACK, LIKE A GIANT HAND SHOVING ME. PIECES OF DEBRIS FELL AROUND ME... AT MY FEET... ON MY SHOULDER. STILL, I DID NOT LOOK BACK.
BEFORE I LEFT I HAD TAKEN MY CAP FROM UNDER MY CHAIR AND REPLACED IT WITH TWO ARMED GRENADES I'D HIDDEN IN MY JACKET POCKETS. I HAD ONLY SECONDS TO LEAVE THE BUILDING.
I LOOKED STRAIGHT AHEAD, BUT I SAW NOTHING. ONLY THE FACES OF THOSE WHO LIVED YET IN MY MIND. MAMA... PAPA... MY SISTER, CHAIYA... AND THE REBBE.

YOSSEL (ibooks inc.)

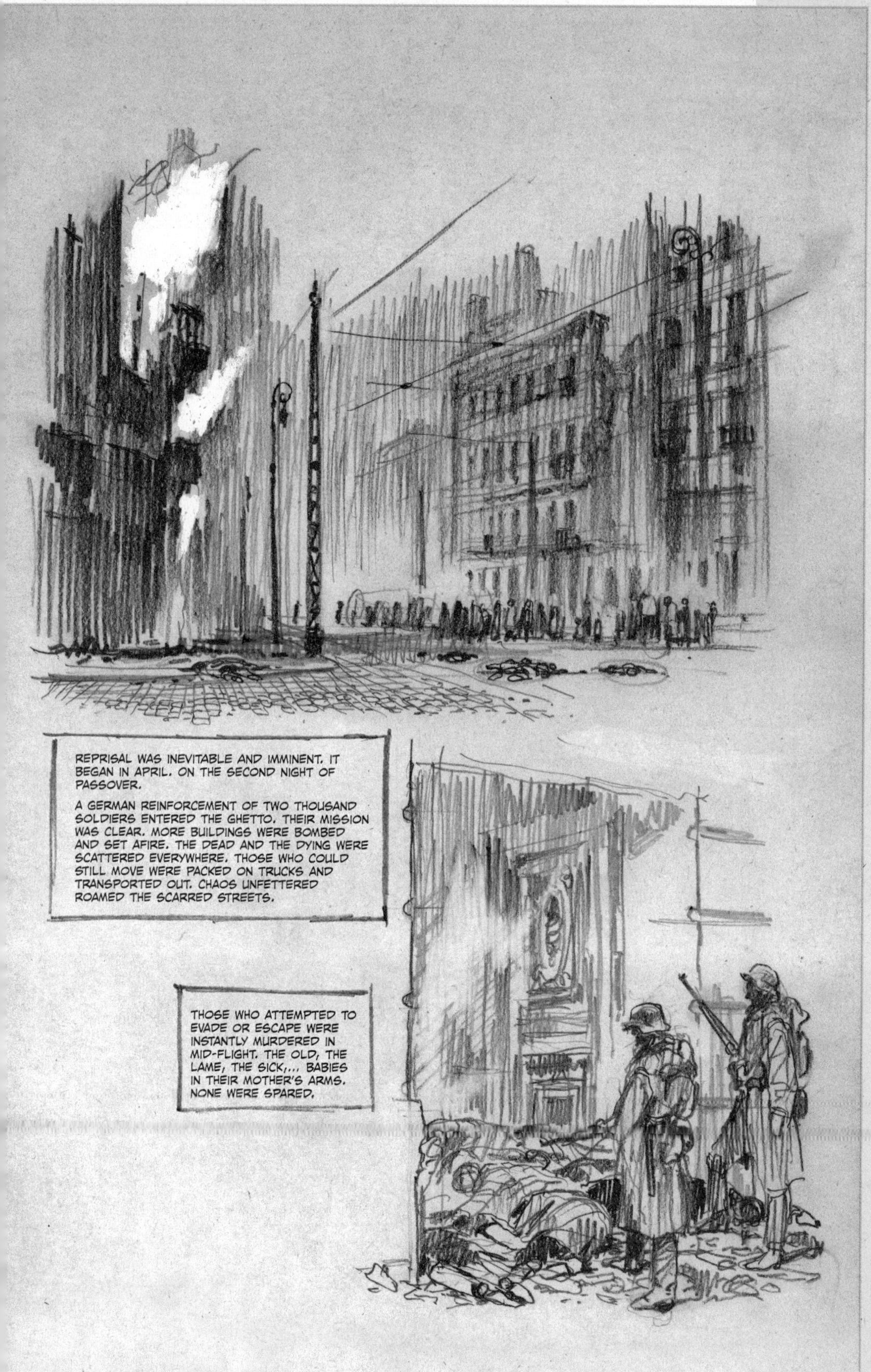

REPRISAL WAS INEVITABLE AND IMMINENT. IT BEGAN IN APRIL. ON THE SECOND NIGHT OF PASSOVER.

A GERMAN REINFORCEMENT OF TWO THOUSAND SOLDIERS ENTERED THE GHETTO. THEIR MISSION WAS CLEAR. MORE BUILDINGS WERE BOMBED AND SET AFIRE. THE DEAD AND THE DYING WERE SCATTERED EVERYWHERE. THOSE WHO COULD STILL MOVE WERE PACKED ON TRUCKS AND TRANSPORTED OUT. CHAOS UNFETTERED ROAMED THE SCARRED STREETS.

THOSE WHO ATTEMPTED TO EVADE OR ESCAPE WERE INSTANTLY MURDERED IN MID-FLIGHT. THE OLD, THE LAME, THE SICK,... BABIES IN THEIR MOTHER'S ARMS. NONE WERE SPARED.

"WE HAVE LEARNED THAT HIMMLER HAS SENT AN ORDER TO LEVEL THE ENTIRE GHETTO. NO STONE IS TO BE LEFT STANDING."
"WHAT WILL THEY DO, MORDECAI... WITH THE PEOPLE?"
"DO? WHAT IS THERE TO DO? THEY WILL SEND US ALL TO THE OVENS."
"NO, RIFKA... NOT THE OVENS. NOT FOR US."
"B-BUT, WHAT CAN WE DO, MORDECAI? WE ARE SO FEW- "
"THERE ARE OTHER GROUPS LIKE US. HERE IN THE GHETTO. WE WILL NOT GIVE UP. WE CAN FIGHT. WE CAN KILL SOME OF THEM. WE CAN DIE LIKE HUMAN BEINGS."

AT 6 AM, ON THE NINETEENTH OF APRIL, 1943, THE GERMAN ASSAULT ON THE WARSAW GHETTO BEGAN.
AT DAWN, WE WERE ON THE ROOF OF OUR BUILDING. EACH OF US CARRIED GUNS, AMMUNITION, GRENADES, KNIVES. ALL WE HAD TAKEN FROM THE SOLDIERS' DEAD BODIES.
A SMOKY HAZE LAY ON THE MORNING AIR, DIMMING THE WEAK SUNLIGHT. THEN WE HEARD THE CLANK AND GRIND OF METAL TREADS AS TANKS APPROACHED THE GHETTO WALL. NOW WE COULD SEE THEM. THE SWASTIKA-ADORNED ARMORED JUGGERNAUTS AND THE SOLDIERS. ROW UPON ROW, MARCHING INTO THE GHETTO.
"I HAVE NEVER SEEN SO MANY SOLDIERS, MORDECAI."
"THAT WILL MAKE EASIER TARGETS FOR US, YOSSEL."
"THEY ARE... COMING INTO... OUR BUILDING."

YOSSEL (ibooks inc.)

OWLY (Top Shelf Productions)

Zzz

OWLY

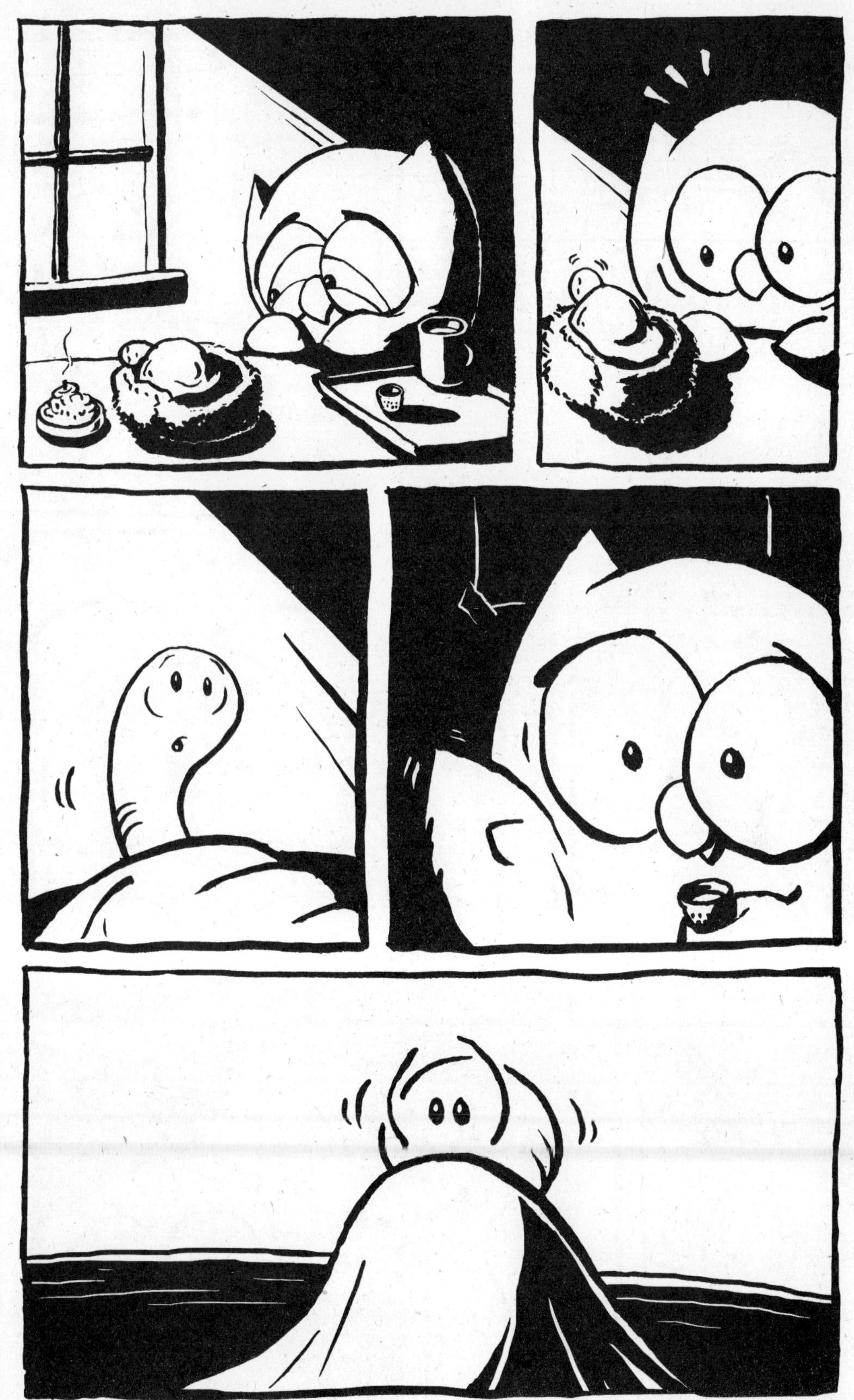

OWLY (Top Shelf Productions)

OWLY (Top Shelf Productions)

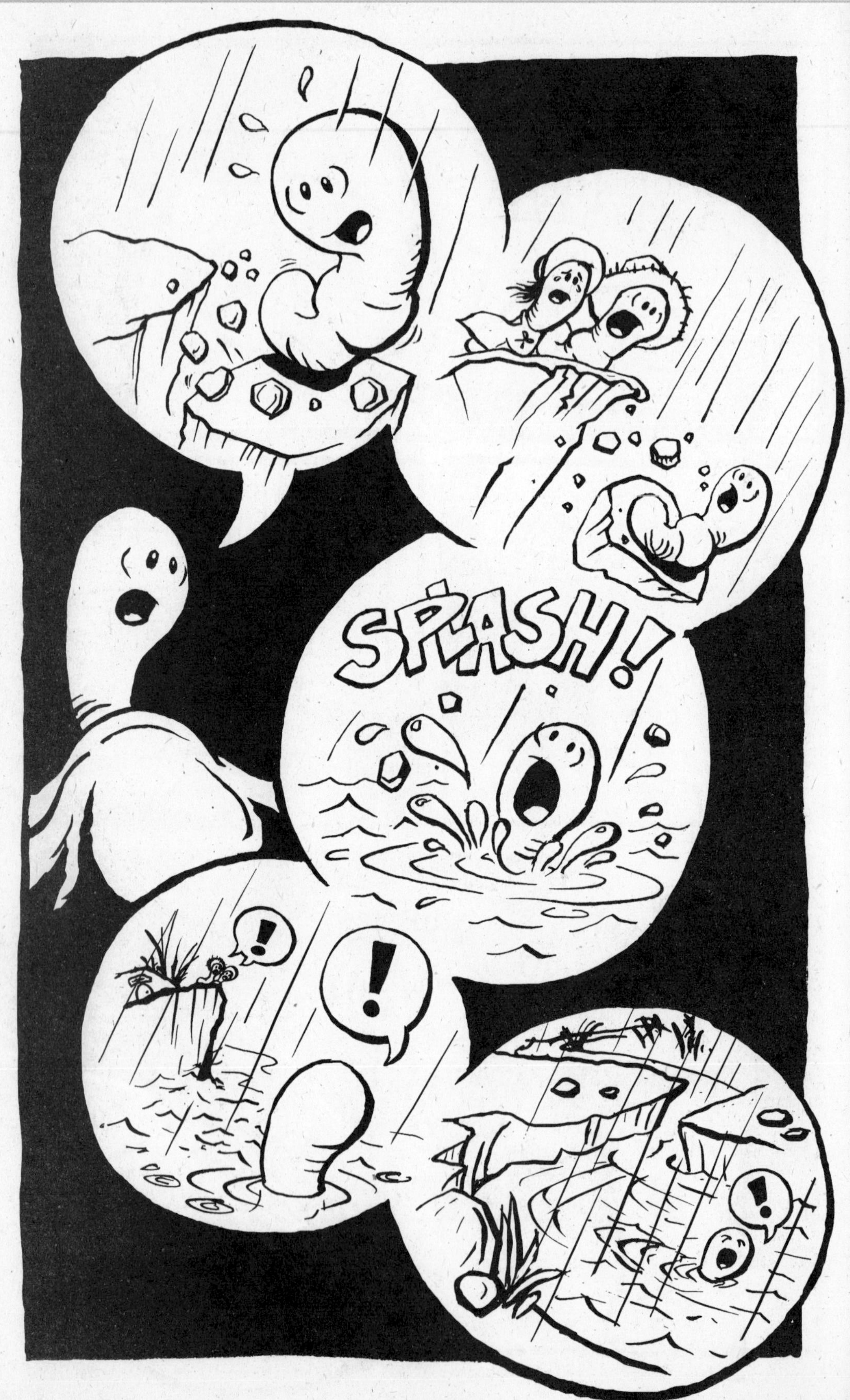
SPLASH!
!
!
!

OWLY (Top Shelf Productions)

?
MAP

You line in.
Yeah, all right. Give me a fucking chance, Lel.
The Dirt'll be down by Weller Street drinking all night.
Huh, I'm not worried about them.
Just shitting yourself, that's all.
It's the Law I don't want to see. Those bastards have got guns now.
What, get shot for spraying up a wall? It's kid stuff.
Anyway, we got enough money for a Hover yet?
THE Originals
DAVE GIBBONS

THE ORIGINALS (Vertigo/DC Comics)

Working on it. These Emms cost nothing, by the time I sold the other half on.
Keep on like that and we'll be rolling in it any day now.
Right, any day now. So how about another couple free, then, Lel?
Originals
All right, seeing as you did such a nice job on the wall!
Originals
Yeah, really nice job, Bok!

Fuck off, Warren.
Hear what the Dirt did?
Pulled one of Ronnie's boys off a Hover!
Yeah, we heard. Now fuck off.
What this needs is a bit more dazzle.
And what you need is a fucking good kicking.
So fuck off out of it before I give you one.
You heard him. Fuck off.
Wanker.

THE ORIGINALS (Vertigo/DC Comics)

Wanker Warren. Remember that time he --
Hovers.
It was them.
Coming our way.

Stopping.
It was them.

The Originals.

THE ORIGINALS (Vertigo/DC Comics)

NEIL GAIMAN • ANDY KUBERT • RICHARD ISANOVE
MARVEL
1602

JSA
ALL STARS

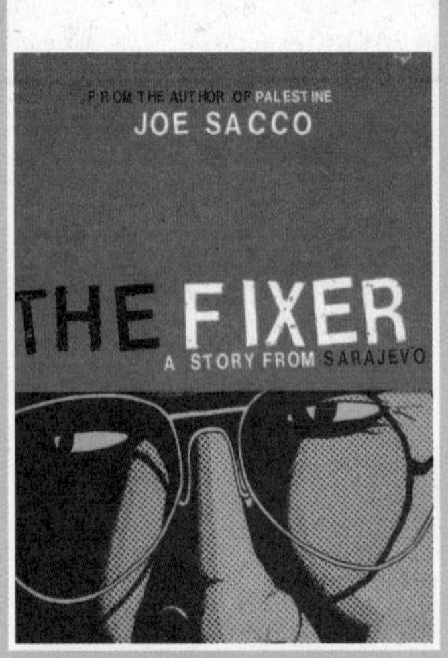
FROM THE AUTHOR OF PALESTINE
JOE SACCO
THE FIXER
A STORY FROM SARAJEVO

COURTNEY CRUMRIN IN THE TWILIGHT KINGDOM

ALAN MOORE
FROM THE PAGES OF THE HIT SERIES TOP 10:
SMAX
ZANDER CANNON
ANDREW CURRIE

LOST AT SEA
BRYAN LEE O'MALLEY

-SPOOKHOUSE-

AMAZE INK
ANTONY MAZZOTTA
BOMBABY
THE SCREEN GODDESS
Sangeeta Mukherjee
Is the reincarnation of Mombai's ancient protector. Can she ever be her own woman?

Nightmares
& Fairy Tales
Once Upon a Time...
by Serena Valentino & FSc

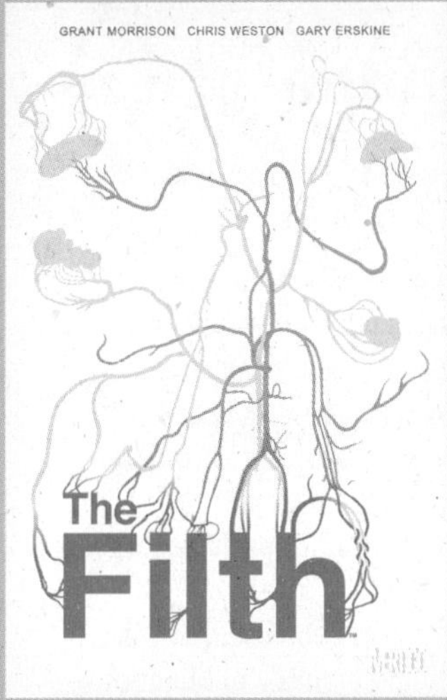
GRANT MORRISON CHRIS WESTON GARY ERSKINE
The Filth

VERTIGO
WE3
GRANT MORRISON
FRANK QUITELY

Grant Morrison
Cameron Stewart
seaguy
VERTIGO

PERSEPOLIS
MARJANE SATRAPI

CLYDE FANS BOOK·1

Tommysaurus Rex
by
Doug TenNapel

singularity
7

SCANDALOUS
J. TORRES • SCOTT CHANTLER

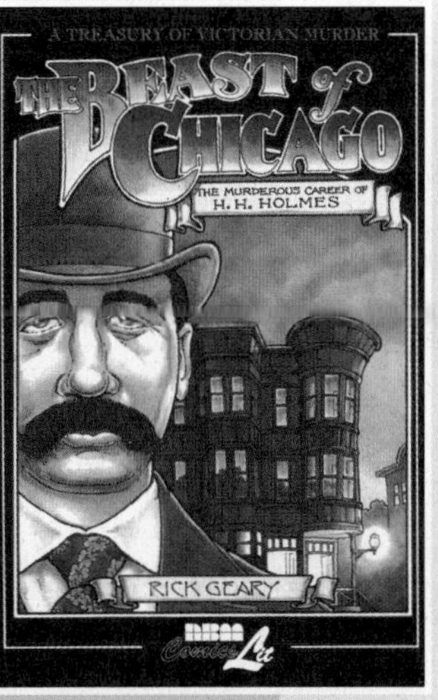
A TREASURY OF VICTORIAN MURDER
THE BEAST of CHICAGO
THE MURDEROUS CAREER OF H. H. HOLMES
RICK GEARY
ComicsLit

Comics

By Greg McElhatton

Single issues of comics are simultaneously the backbone of the comics industry and an endangered species. There's no denying that for over half a century the periodical form has been the delivery standard. Bags, boards, and long boxes are the tools of the collector's trade, and you can buy specially quality-graded and sealed issues from companies whose sole purpose is to determine the level of a comic's pristine condition. Most comic specialty stores gain the bulk of their profits—and pay the rent—through the selling of periodicals.

But the rise of graphic novels as a market force has shifted attention away from the traditional monthly format. Deciding to wait for a collected edition is now the rule for many rather than the exception. Additionally, many publishers have abandoned or heavily shifted away from single issues of comics.

The sad thing is that, even as all of this occurs, some of the most exciting comics published in the last year are in this original format. Joss Whedon, John Cassaday, and Laura Martin's *The Astonishing X-Men* was a regular dose of pure excitement, introducing new villains and reviving old characters in 32-page installments. In many ways, their first six-issue storyline could be used as a primer on how to craft a popular ongoing comic. It's also hard to argue against the strength of a book as perfect as Eric Shanower's *Age of Bronze*. A retelling of the Trojan War, every issue features iconic covers that pop off the stands, and meticulously crafted interior art that is as lush and provocative as the story it's presenting.

Bringing old characters and stories to life is a trait more often seen in periodicals than graphic novels. From the unexpectedly fantastic revival of *Conan* by Kurt Busiek and Cary Nord, to Kyle Baker's crazy take on *Plastic Man*, periodicals can be used as a testing ground to see if the market is ready to see familiar faces again. A project like Darwyn Cooke's 400-page DC: *The New Frontier* might have been daunting to potential customers, but in six 64-page installments it's easier to give it a chance.

Periodicals can build up momentum and excitement for an "event." Books like *Identity Crisis*, showing up over seven months, were able to get reactions out of readers in a way that a single volume couldn't.

Last but not least, periodicals are a place for slightly different, off-beat, or more obscure titles to experiment and build an audience. You can use the format to tell stories about a homeless skateboarding girl who fights ninjas, or twelve unconnected tales of super-powered teenagers, or an American expatriate living in Mexico City, or an aboriginal tracker who makes his way through life in a world containing elements of both our past and future. Jim Rugg and Brian Maruca's *Street Angel*, Brian Wood and Becky Cloonan's *Demo*, Jessica Abel's *La Perdida*, and Carla Speed McNeil's *Finder* are all books that were able to gain

Table of Contents

buzz and popularity over time through serialization even as their creators continued to shape and refine their craft. While all these books have "graphic novel collections" published or scheduled, it was through their initial editions as periodicals that they were able to make a splash.

Graphic novels may be the wave of the future, but the comics in this book will show you that there are still great things to be found in this time-honored format.

17TH AND STONE ST.
AEGNAP AUTO REPAIR
PRIVATE PROPERTY
NO TRESPASSING
BEWARE OF DOG

NINJA
OGER

SLIDE.

WHRRRRRRRRRRRRRRRRRRR

PANGEA'S LAIR IS A LETHAL COMBINATION OF MUSCLE AND THE MECHANICAL. IT'S A REMOTE CONTROL DEATH HOUSE RIGGED TO TRACK AND DESTROY ANY UNWELCOME INTRUDERS.

STREET ANGEL (Slave Labor Graphics)

SOMETIMES IT'S GOOD TO BE 5'1".
DEADLY STARS.
NINJA GUARDS.
SWORDS.
ARROWS.
LASERS.
PIZZL!
FZZZLLPP
BOMBS!?! WHAT THE HELL WAS THAT?!?
BOOM

STREET ANGEL (Slave Labor Graphics)

IRRITATED, STREET ANGEL TRIUMPHANTLY SURVEYS THE WAREHOUSE.
WHERE'S MY SHOE?

COME ON!
STUPID DOOR! OPEN!
JUST LIKE A NINJA TO LOCK UP BEFORE A FIGHT.
HOPE THERE AREN'T ANY FAN BLADES ON THE OTHER END.

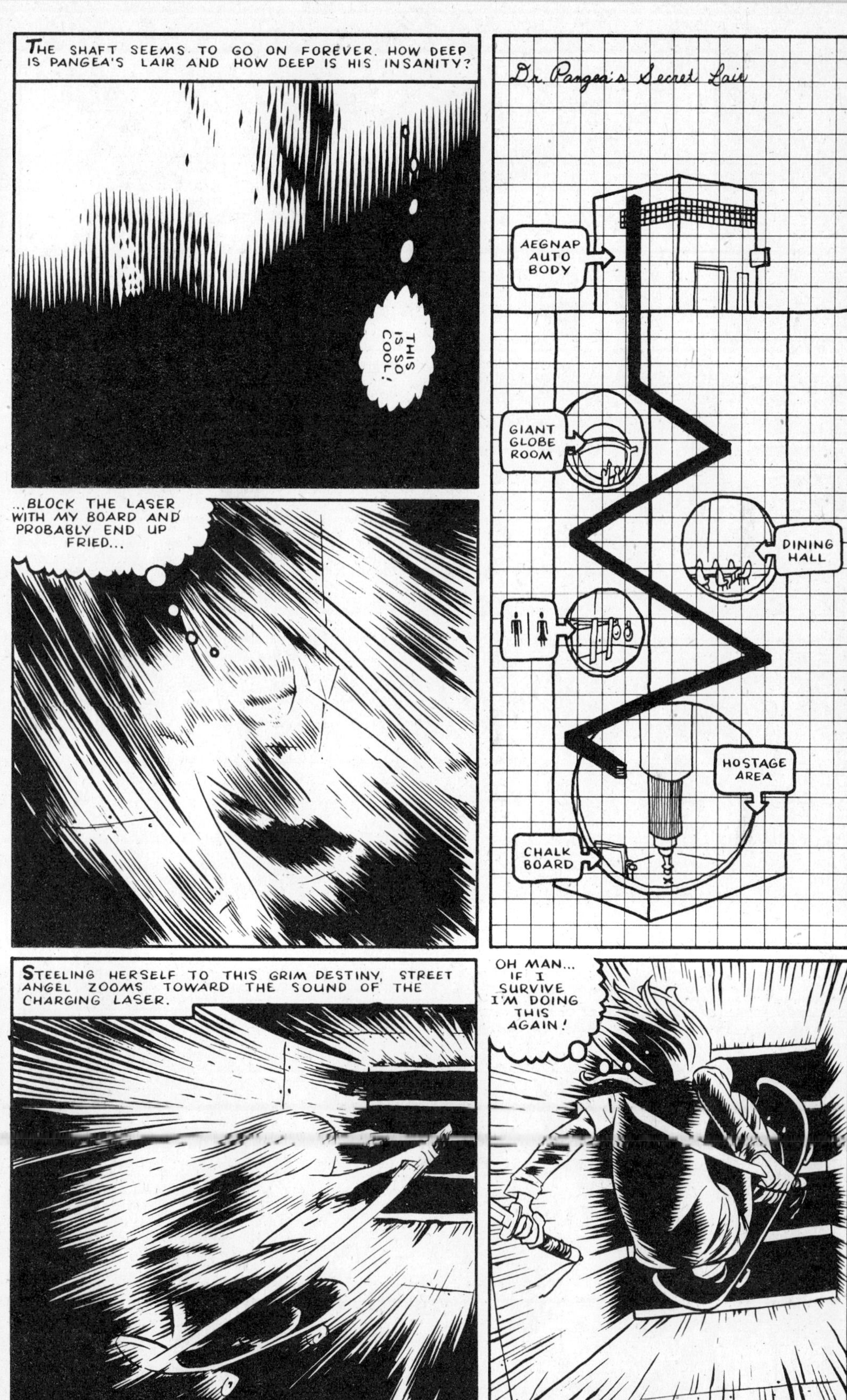
THE SHAFT SEEMS TO GO ON FOREVER. HOW DEEP IS PANGEA'S LAIR AND HOW DEEP IS HIS INSANITY?
THIS IS SO COOL!
Dr. Pangea's Secret Lair
AEGNAP AUTO BODY
GIANT GLOBE ROOM
DINING HALL
HOSTAGE AREA
CHALK BOARD
...BLOCK THE LASER WITH MY BOARD AND PROBABLY END UP FRIED...
STEELING HERSELF TO THIS GRIM DESTINY, STREET ANGEL ZOOMS TOWARD THE SOUND OF THE CHARGING LASER.
OH MAN... IF I SURVIVE I'M DOING THIS AGAIN!

STREET ANGEL (Slave Labor Graphics)

STREET ANGEL!
BONG
AW CRAP!
POP

THE PROBLEM WITH A CELESTIALLY TIME-BASED PLAN IS THAT YOU ONLY GET ONE SHOT.
MALFUNCTION! MALFUNCTION! MALF
NO. NO! NOOO!
OOF!
CTION! MALFUNCTION! MALFUNCTION! MALFUNCTION! MALFUNCTION! MALFUNCTION! MALFUNCTION! MALFUN

THIS CAN'T BE HAPPENING...

IT WILL TAKE AN HOUR TO REBOOT THE...

...MY ELABORATE, FOOL-PROOF ...PLAN...
THUD!
MALFUNCTION! MALFUNCTION! MALFUNCTION! MALFUNCTION! MALFUNCTION! MALFUNCTION! MALFUNCTION!

I'M NOT DEAD! I'M NOT DE--
OH RIGHT, NINJAS!

STREET ANGEL (Slave Labor Graphics)

It ain't that hard, Wooz! You just gotta march to the beat of your own drum!

Lay down your own funk and make 'em dance!

Easy for you to say, Plas...

But dames just don't go for a guy like me.

Nonsense! I know for a fact that the ladies love a softie!

DRIVING the GOILS WOOZY
STORY & ART BY SCOTT MORSE
LETTERED BY ROB LEIGH
EDITED BY JOEY CAVALIERI

PLASTC MAN (DC Comics)

Chez Amour
Just look at the selection, Woozy, my boy!

This place is HOPPIN', pal!

I got only so much love to give, Wooz... you better get down here an' back me up!

PLASTC MAN (DC Comics)

I don't know...

Slide on down, we gotta talk this through.

Now tell me, what is it you look for in a lady?
What makes the Wooz give up the wuv?
Hmmm... well, you know, a pulse...

That's genius, Wooz! Comedy!
A funny opening line will work MIRACLES in a place like this!

Lay out yer cards, pardner. What's yer big line? Betcha got an ace up yer sleeve...

Umm... all right... How's... ummm...

Er, no, WAIT! YEAH! How's thi-- No, no, that's dumb. Hold on. Umm...

Oh, COME ON, man!
You can DO this!

PLASTC MAN (DC Comics)

Pay attention, now, soldier!
You gotta line 'em up in yer cross hairs an' fire away!
We're goin' in! I'll be your wingman, in case you need someone to run interference!
Good luck!
PLOP!

PLASTC MAN (DC Comics)

'Scuse me, ma'am, clan I dry you some plink?

Er, try you to THINK?

Drive you to... to...

...to...

PLASTIC MAN (DC Comics)

DAUGHTER OF TYNDAREUS, HAVE YOU SPOKEN TO YOUR HUSBAND?
HE WON'T SAVE HER. BUT THE ARMY--?
KALCHAS HAS REVEALED **EVERYTHING** TO AN ARMY OF MEN CRAZY WITH IMPATIENCE TO REACH TROY. EVEN MY OWN MEN ARE SHOUTING FOR YOUR DAUGHTER.
SHSHSHSHSHSHSHSHSHSHSHSHSHSHSHSHSHSHSHSHSHSHS
WON'T ANYONE HELP US?
THERE'S NO TIME TO FIND OUT! YOU'VE GOT TO LEAVE AULIS **NOW!**
HE'S BLEEDING!
WHERE ARE YOUR CHARIOTS?
THE CHARIOTS --I DON'T KNOW!
THEN WE'LL HAVE TO TAKE THE FIRST ONES WE FIND.
AGE OF BRONZE
image
SACRIFICE 10
SHSHSHSHSHSHSHSHSHSHSHSHSHSHSHSHSHSHSHSHSHSH
OH! IS HE COMING WITH US?
SOMEONE MUST DEFEND YOU!
AGAINST THE WHOLE ARMY?
I DON'T HAVE ANOTHER CHOICE! MY HONOR IS TIED TO YOUR DAUGHTER!
SHSHSHSHSHSHSHSHSHSHSHSHSHSHSHSHSHSHSHSHSHSHS

AGE OF BRONZE (Image Comics/Hungry Tiger Press)

HERE THEY COME.
THIS SPEAR WILL DRINK ALL THE BLOOD IT CAN. ONCE I'M DEAD, WRAP YOUR ARMS AROUND HER--THEY WON'T BE ABLE TO DRAG HER AWAY SO EASILY.
OH, GREAT MOTHER--
LET'S
WAIT!
SHSHSHSHSHSHSHSHSHSHSHSHSHSHSHSHSHSH
DON'T THROW YOUR LIFE AWAY, SON OF PELEUS! NOT FOR ME--I'M NOTHING--
YOU'RE THE HIGH KING'S DAUGHTER!
IPHIGENIA!
SHSHSHSHSHSHSHSHSHSHSHSH
THE GODDESS WANTS MY LIFE. ONLY MINE. NO ONE ELSE NEEDS TO DIE. NOT MY MOTHER. NOT MY FATHER. NOT YOU, SON OF PELEUS.
YOU'RE SO GOOD AND BRAVE. MY FATHER WILL NEED YOU AT TROY.
DON'T WASTE YOUR LIFE FOR ME.
SHSHSHSHSHSHSHSHSHSHSHSH
IPHIGENIA!
I WON'T LET YOU DIE FOR ME. I'LL GO TO ARTEMIS ALONE!
GET UP! GET UP! WE'VE GOT TO LEAVE!
SHSHSHSHSHSHSHSHSHSHSHSHSHSHSHSHSHSH

YOU DON'T KNOW WHAT YOU'RE SAYING--
YES, I DO, MOTHER! LISTEN!
THERE'S NO TIME FOR THIS!
NO...
THEY'LL KILL ME ANYWAY ONCE HE'S DEAD! I CAN'T ESCAPE! LET MY DEATH MEAN SOMETHING! LET ME SAVE MY HUSBAND!
WHAT?
NO!
SON OF PELEUS, I WISH I REALLY COULD CALL YOU MY HUSBAND. YOU'D GIVE YOUR LIFE FOR ME-- LET ME GIVE MINE FOR YOU.
NOT ONLY THAT--MY LIFE WILL SEND THE ARMY TO TROY--A GIFT TO ALL THOSE THOUSANDS WILLING TO GIVE THEIR OWN LIVES. YOU'LL CONQUER TROY BECAUSE OF ME, BRING BACK MY AUNT AND LITTLE PLEISTHENES. I'LL BE PART OF THIS WHOLE, HUGE, AMAZING THING.
MY LIFE WILL GIVE GLORY TO ALL OUR PEOPLE...
GIVE YOU GLORY ...ACHILLES.

AGE OF BRONZE (Image Comics/Hungry Tiger Press)

NO! NO!
WAIT! I HAVE SOMETHING TO SAY TO YOUR DAUGHTER.
DAUGHTER OF AGAMEMNON, YOUR NOBLE WORDS... I **WILL** MARRY YOU...
I...
SHSHSHSHSHSH
IPHIGENIA!
SHSHSHSHSHSH
NO MARRIAGE... NOTHING MORE FOR ME...
SHSHSHSHSHSH
ONLY GLORY...
GLORY, YES... I UNDERSTAND.
I WON'T STAND IN THE WAY OF YOUR ONE GREAT DEED.
THANK YOU, ACHILLES...
BUT IF YOU CHANGE YOUR MIND--EVEN AS THE KNIFE DESCENDS--**ONE LOOK** FROM YOU AND I'LL SAVE YOU.
...JUST... REMEMBER ME...
REMEMBER-- ONE LOOK!
SHSHSHSHSHSH

DON'T CRY, MOTHER! OR I'LL CRY, TOO.
OH, MY BABY-Y-Y... HOW CAN THIS BE HAP-HAPPENING?... LET THEM TAKE SOMEONE ELSE'S DAUGHTER--FIND SOME OTHER GIRL...
GOOD-BYE, MOTHER. PLEASE DO ONE THING FOR ME. DON'T HATE FATHER. DON'T HATE HIM.
TRAMP TRAMP TRAMP TRAMP TRAMP TRAMP
IMPOSSIBLE!
IT'S NOT HIS FAULT. HE CAN'T DEFY THE GODS.
MOTHER, KISS ME ONE LAST TIME-- HOLD ME...
I'LL HOLD YOU... HOLD YOU TIGHT LIKE ACHILLES SAID. THEY'LL HAVE TO KILL ME TO GET TO YOU.
TRAMP TRAMP TRAMP TRAMP TRAMP TRAMP
NO, MOTHER, MY SISTERS BACK IN MYCENAE-- THEY NEED YOU.
AND MY BROTHER NEEDS YOU, TOO, NEEDS YOU TO BE STRONG, MOTHER, TO MAKE HIM STRONG.
GOOD-BYE, ORESTES. REMEMBER ME WHEN YOU'RE A MAN. I HOPE YOU AND MOTHER WILL TALK ABOUT ME SOMETIMES, TALK ONLY ABOUT THE SWEET MEMORIES--TO BRING EACH OTHER JOY.
DAUGHTER OF AGAMEMNON, COME OUT!
TRAMP

GOOD-BYE, ARSINOE. I USED TO HANG ON YOUR NECK LIKE THIS WHEN I WAS LITTLE.
NOW IT'S TIME FOR ME TO GO.
YOU'RE TOO *YOUNG* TO KNOW WHAT YOU'RE *DOING!*
SHSHSHSHSHSHSHSHSHSHSHSHSHSHSHSHSHSHSHSHS
DON'T DISGRACE ME, MOTHER.
THE GODDESS IS CALLING.
LET ME GO TO HER.
SHSHSHSHSHSHSHSHSHSHSHSHSHSHSHSHSHSHSHSH
SHSHSHSHSHSHSHSHSHSHSHSHSHSHSHSHSHSHSHS
SHSHSHSHSHSHSHSHSHSHSHSHSHSHSHSHSHSHSHSHSHSH
THE WIND...
THE WIND STOPPED...
IT STOPPED BLOWING...

AGE OF BRONZE (Image Comics/Hungry Tiger Press)

LEAVE ME ALONE!

AGE OF BRONZE (Image Comics/Hungry Tiger Press)

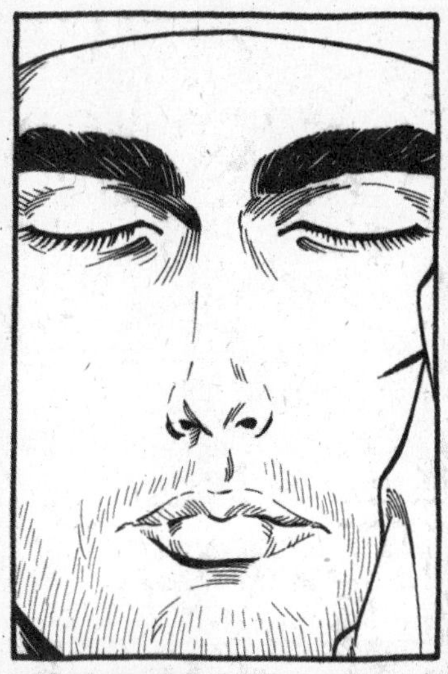

YES...

...FOR TROY TO FALL, THE FIRST-BORN DAUGHTER OF AGAMEMNON MUST DIE.

I'M BOUND BY HONOR TO RESCUE HER IF SHE ASKS ME TO, MOTHER.

IF YOU RESCUE HER, YOU WON'T SAIL FOR TROY. THAT'S WHAT I'VE WANTED ALL ALONG... BUT NOW-- I FEAR A BATTLE AT THE ALTAR.
MOTHER, DEATH LIES IN WAIT FOR *EVERYONE*.

YOUR DEATH WILL COME FROM THE SUN GOD IN RETRIBUTION FOR YOUR SLAYING A SON OF HIS.
I HAVEN'T SLAIN ONE YET.

I CAN MAKE SURE YOU NEVER DO.
MNEMON, COME HERE.

AGE OF BRONZE (Image Comics/Hungry Tiger Press)

MNEMON CAN RECOGNIZE THE SUN GOD'S CHILDREN. FROM NOW ON HE'LL ACCOMPANY YOU INTO BATTLE TO STEER YOU AWAY FROM EVERY SON OF THE GOD.
CAN YOU FIGHT, MNEMON?

I'LL FIGHT WELL FOR YOU, SON OF THE NEREID, AND KEEP YOU SAFE.
VERY GOOD ANSWER.

THEN PUT ON ARMOR AND GET READY FOR BATTLE.
BUT WE WON'T FACE THE SUN GOD TONIGHT. THE GIRL IS CLAIMED BY ARTEMIS OF THE HUNT, THE MOON GODDESS.

TAKE MY BLESSING WITH YOU, ALL OF YOU...
THANK YOU, MOTHER.

LET'S GO!

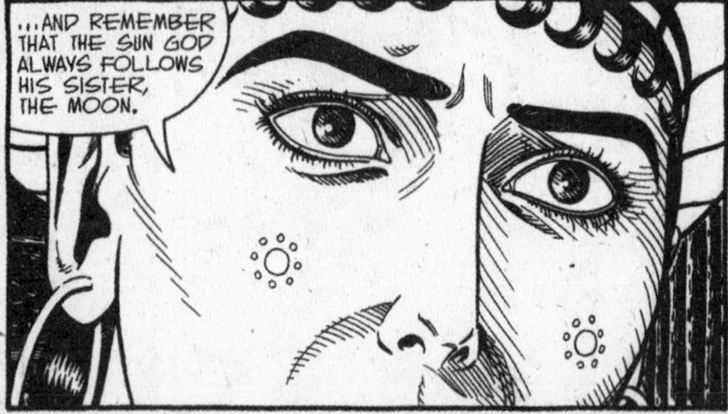
...AND REMEMBER THAT THE SUN GOD ALWAYS FOLLOWS HIS SISTER, THE MOON.

AGE OF BRONZE (Image Comics/Hungry Tiger Press)

ALL RIGHT, I THINK THIS IS YOUR STOP, LADY.
WHAT KIND OF PSEUDONYM IS *HUNDRED*, ANYWAY?
FOR THE LAST TIME, I AM A *THIRTEENTH-* GENERATION AMERICAN.
MY ANCESTORS RENAMED THEMSELVES AFTER *BRANDYWINE* HUNDRED, THE DIVISION OF DELAWARE WHERE THEY SETTLED.
AND UNLESS YOU CAN PROVE TO ME THAT MYLES STANDISH--CAPTAIN OF THE FUCKING *MAYFLOWER*--WAS AN ALIEN, I'M DONE ANSWERING RETARDED QUESTIONS ABOUT MY *PLANET OF ORIGIN*.
NO OFFENSE, SIR, I APPRECIATE WHAT YOU DID FOR THIS CITY AND ALL... BUT I SEE WHY MY PAPER DIDN'T *ENDORSE* YOU.
WELL, NO OFFENSE, BUT I SEE WHY YOUR PAPER IS *FREE*.
LET'S ROLL, BRADBURY.
EX MACHINA
THE FIRST HUNDRED DAYS
BRIAN K. VAUGHAN TONY HARRIS TOM FEISTER
AHH, *SHIT!*
SHE'S GONNA QUOTE ME ON "RETARDED," ISN'T SHE?
YEP.
STILL, I'D BANG THAT GIRL LIKE A *SCREEN DOOR*.
YOU KNOW, BRADBURY, NINE DAYS OUT OF TEN, I REALLY WISH YOU AND I HAD NEVER *MET*...
SHARKY LARUE
SALEEM'S HOT FISH

EX MACHINA (Wildstorm Productions)

THIS COULDN'T HAVE WAITED UNTIL TOMORROW, CAPTAIN BRADBURY?

MONDAY, OCTOBER 18, 1999

HAVEN'T BEEN A CAPTAIN SINCE I LEFT THE MARINES, MR. HUNDRED. SIGNING UP WITH THE HARBOR PATROL BUSTED ME DOWN TO A LOWLY LIEUTENANT.

OH, I, UH, THOUGHT EVERYONE WHO DROVE A BOAT WAS CALLED--

AND *NO,* THIS COULDN'T HAVE WAITED.

POLICE NEW YORK CITY

I SPOTTED SOMETHING... ***WEIRD*** DURING MY LAST SHIFT. COAST GUARD SAID IT WASN'T THEIR JURISDICTION, TOLD ME TO CALL ONE OF THE CITY'S ***CIVIL ENGINEERS.***

GAL WHO ANSWERED THE PHONE SAID YOU KNEW MORE ABOUT IT THAN ANYBODY ALIVE.

MORE ABOUT ***WHAT,*** LIEUTENANT?

IT.
AH... THE OLD BITCH.
SORRY?
SOME OF MY COLLEAGUES ARE A LITTLE SUPERSTITIOUS ABOUT THE BROOKLYN BRIDGE. IT'S ALWAYS BEEN BAD LUCK FOR CIVIL ENGINEERS.
POLICE
THE ONE WHO DESIGNED IT DIED FROM TETANUS AFTER AN ACCIDENT ON THE PILINGS. AND HIS SON GOT A FATAL CASE OF THE BENDS FROM WORKING UNDERWATER ON THE--
--FOUNDATIONS?
YEAH, THAT'S WHERE I SAW SOMETHING GLOWING.
WHAT?
AND YOU DIDN'T CALL THE BOMB SQUAD? OR THE--
I WORKED DEMOLITIONS FOR NINE YEARS, SIR. THIS AIN'T A BOMB. BESIDES, IT'S NOT ATTACHED TO THE BRIDGE, LOOKS MORE LIKE IT'S GROWING OUT OF IT.
PATROLMAN RICK A BRADBURY
NEW YORK CITY
No 2
HERE, TAKE A LOOK FOR YOURSELF...

GOOD SHOOTING, HATFIELD!

JESUS CHRIST! YER A FUCKING NATURAL!

I HATE THIS.

BLAM

I HATE THIS.

THP!

"Intense and profound... mind-blowing" - Wizard
BRIAN WOOD / BECKY CLOONAN
DEMO
#7: One Shot, Don't Miss

DEMO (AiT/Planet Lar)

FIRST DAY OUT, HATFIELD?

WELL, YEAH. I'VE BEEN HERE A COUPLE WEEKS, BUT THIS IS MY FIRST DAY ON PATROL.

FEELIN' THE *HEAT*?
HA HA!

HERE, LEMME HELP YOU WITH THAT SHIT.
DON'T I NEED THAT?

DEMO (AiT/Planet Lar)

NAH, THESE ARE THE OLD ONES. ALL THEY DO IS MAKE YOU SWEAT. ANY DECENT SHOT FROM AN AK'LL GO RIGHT THROUGH IT.
BETTER TO NOT HAVE IT AND STAY ON YOUR TOES THAN TRUST IT TO SAVE YOUR LIFE.
CLANG

WE SHOULD BE GETTING THE NEW ONES "ANY DAY NOW."

YOUR BEST DEFENSE IS A STRONG OFFENSE ANYWAY. JUST KEEP YOUR EYES PEELED FOR INCOMING VEHICLES.
ANY CAR COMING HERE KNOWS TO STOP. THEY SEE THE SIGNS, THEY SEE THE BARRIER, AND THEY SEE US POINTING OUR WEAPONS. THEY KNOW THEY GOTTA STOP.
IF THEY DON'T STOP, WE GOTTA ASSUME IT'S HOSTILE AND THEY GOT WEAPONS, MAYBE A BOMB. WE SHOOT FIRST, WE TAKE 'EM OUT.

WHAT, LIKE, DISABLE THE VEHICLE?

NO, FUCKHEAD, SHOOT TO KILL. TAKE THE WHOLE FUCKING THING OUT.
THAT'S WHY YOU'RE HERE, AIN'T IT?

BESIDES, I HEAR YOU ARE ONE HOT-SHIT SHOT, YOU NEVER MISS.
SOME KINDA BORN-WITH-A-RIFLE-IN-HIS-HAND FARM BOY?

YEAH, SOMETHING LIKE THAT. I DON'T MISS TOO OFTEN.
I HEAR YOU DON'T MISS EVER.

YEAH, NOT TOO OFTEN, NO.
THEY RECRUITED ME PRETTY HARD BECAUSE OF IT. MY HIGH SCHOOL COACH GAVE THEM MY NUMBER. HE USED TO HUNT WITH ME AND MY OLD MAN.

SO WHAT WAS IT THAT GOT YOU? THE "EARN AN EXTRA PAYCHECK?" OR THE "ONE WEEKEND A MONTH?"
"EARN MONEY FOR COLLEGE." IT'S THE ONLY WAY I CAN AFFORD IT.

COPY THAT, "CITIZEN-SOLDIER." I THOUGHT I'D BE PUTTING OUT FOREST FIRES AND DRIVING HUMVEES AROUND, NOT SWEATING LIKE A FUCKING PIG HALFWAY AROUND THE WORLD FOR THE LAST SIX MONTHS.
NO SHIT, ME TOO.

COLLEGE BETTER BE FUCKING WORTH IT.

HEADS UP! WE GOT INCOMING.

FUCK.

HERE WE GO AGAIN. EVERYONE GET READY!

GET YOUR RIFLE UP, HATFIELD!

DEMO (AiT/Planet Lar)

HE'S STOPPING.
WHAT THE FUCK? COME ON! COME ON!

WHAT DO YOU THINK IT MEANS?
MAYBE SCARED, MAYBE NOT...

HATFIELD! YOU HANG BACK AND COVER US.

OH, FUCK.

REEEE

HATFIELD! TAKE HIM OUT NOW!

WE CAN'T FIRE, WE CAN'T SEE YOU! IT'S UP TO YOU! KILL HIM NOW!

I can't do this, I can't kill someone. I can't shoot at this person. I'll kill him.

FIRE NOW!

BLAM

SKREE
VRRRR

WHAT THE FUCK, HATFIELD? YOU NOT HEAR US?
YOU MISSED? FROM SIX FEET AWAY? I TOLD YOU TO SHOOT THE DRIVER, NOT HIS FUCKING TIRES.
NAH, HE DIDN'T MISS.
HE NEVER MISSES. RIGHT, HATFIELD?
FUCKING PUSSY.

CARE TO EXPLAIN YOUR ACTIONS TODAY, HATFIELD?
SIR.
I DON'T THINK I SHOULD BE HERE, SIR.
I WAS RECRUITED BECAUSE OF MY ABILITY TO KILL, BUT THAT'S NOT WHAT I SIGNED UP FOR.
DO YOU HONESTLY THINK ANY OF THAT IS YOUR DECISION TO MAKE, AT THIS POINT? DO YOU UNDERSTAND THE SITUATION YOU ARE IN, HATFIELD?
SIR, MAY I SPEAK FREELY?
GO AHEAD.
THEY SAY I CAN'T MISS WHAT I SHOOT AT. THAT'S PRETTY MUCH TRUE, IT'S ALWAYS BEEN TRUE. IT'S WHAT MAKES ME A VALUABLE SOLDIER, I'M TOLD.
I JUST WONDER WHAT MAKES PEOPLE ASSUME I'M ALWAYS GOING TO BE AIMING AT THE ENEMY?

DEMO (AiT/Planet Lar)

BIGBY!
HE *MADE* IT!
BIGBY! GOD *BLESS* YOUR MOST TIMELY ARRIVAL!
I HAVE TO CONFESS I *NEVER* THOUGHT I'D BE SO PLEASED TO SEE YOU, YOU OLD DOG.
TIME LATER FOR CELEBRATIONS.
WE'VE GOT TOO MUCH *WORK* TO DO.
DIVIDE INTO THREE TEAMS.
YELLOWBRICK ROADHOUSE

FABLES (Vertigo/DC Comics)

YOU CAME!
MISS WHITE?
THE FIRST TEAM FIGHTS THE FIRES STILL BURNING IN THE BUILDINGS, WHERE THE RAINFALL CAN'T GET TO THEM.
I'LL TAKE THAT ONE. FIRE-FIGHTERS, FORM ON ME!
THE SECOND TEAM GATHERS OUR WOUNDED AND GETS THEM INSIDE.
MISS WHITE?
YOU FORGOT YOUR CANE, MISS WHITE.
AND THE THIRD GROUP INSPECTS THE WOODEN SOLDIERS. EXAMINE EACH ONE CAREFULLY.
MAKE SURE THEIR HEADS ARE REMOVED, NO MATTER HOW DEAD THEY MAY SEEM.
CHATEAU D'IF FENCING ACADEMY
WE'LL DO THAT--COLLECT THE HEADS.
STORE THEM INSIDE, IN ONE OF THE ROOMS OFF THE BUSINESS OFFICE--FAR AWAY FROM THEIR BODIES.
BIGBY!

FABLES (Vertigo/DC Comics)

I KNEW IT.
SNOW?
I KNEW YOU'D COME IN TIME TO SAVE US!
YOU ALWAYS DO!
MISS WHITE!
GOLLY!

FABLES (Vertigo/DC Comics)

COMICS

YOU *ALWAYS* SAVE ME.

SNOW, I'M TICKLED TO SEE YOU, TOO, BUT IT'S RAINING CATS AND DOGS AND YOU'RE *PREGNANT.*

THINK OF THE CUB. GET YOURSELF INDOORS THIS *INSTANT.*

WOW! DID YOU SEE *THAT?*

FLY, TAKE SNOW BACK INSIDE.

MY SISTER IS SUDDENLY SO TOTALLY-- ANIMAL.

NOW, PEOPLE, LET'S GET BACK TO WORK. THE *BATTLE* MAY BE OVER, BUT NOT THE *FIGHT.*

WHO'D'VE EVER GUESSED?

FABLES (Vertigo/DC Comics)

THURSDAY, MARCH 28TH. JUST AFTER TWO IN THE MORNING.
THE LONG NIGHT WEARS ON.
DID YOU SEE THAT, FLYCATCHER?
A LIGHTNING STRIKE, BUT REAL CLOSE THIS TIME. MAYBE ON OUR OWN ROOF.
DO YOU THINK WE SHOULD CHECK IT OUT?
STAY HERE. HOLD THE ELEVATOR.
I'LL *INVESTIGATE.*
CAREFUL, YOUR HONOR.
WHAT *IS* THAT?
IS SOMEONE *OUT* THERE?

FABLES (Vertigo/DC Comics)

OH NO.
DEAR GOD, ABOVE.
FLY!
DOWN! PUSH DOWN!
WE NEED TO GO DOWNSTAIRS RIGHT NOW!
WHAT IS IT, SIR? WHAT DID YOU SEE?
SOMETHING? I MEAN, NOTHING! NEVER MIND!
AND NO ONE GOES BACK UP THERE FOR THE REST OF THE NIGHT! THAT'S AN ORDER!

FABLES (Vertigo/DC Comics)

5 am... the "speculum darkroom" nightclub.

SHERIFF LOIS McCREEDY C.P.D.

YUP.

...so the guy turned into a vampire or whatever and tess shot at him with this big stupid holy water cannon she made. but that just sorta pissed him off worse so, um... well, i dunno why i thought of a pony right then, but that's what i conjured up. it swallowed him whole and he's still in there, i guess.

that pony's not very sturdy, though. it'll start to dissolve in about an hour or so.

YEAH, WELL IT'S AN SSI* PROBLEM NOW.

THEY'LL BE HERE WITHIN THE HOUR.

OUR BUDDY HERE GETS LOOSE BEFORE THEN, WE GOT ENOUGH SILVER-TIP ROUNDS IN HERE TO LIGHT THAT SUCKER UP LIKE A TIFFANY'S DISPLAY.

I'D JUST AS SOON PUT HIM OUTTA HIS MISERY RIGHT NOW, BUT YOU KNOW HOW THE FEDS ARE.

yeah...

...but maybe they can, um... y'know... fix... him.

...YOU'RE SHITTIN' ME, RIGHT?

uh...

*ssi = supernatural shield initiative. sort of the fbi of spookystuff.

serenity rose 3

HOME OF THE HEART SHAPED SKULL

SERENITY ROSE (Slave Labor Graphics)

YOU DON'T COME BACK FROM PUMPIN' THAT MUCH CURSE INTO Y'NECK. 'SPECIALLY NOT THE WAY THIS SHIT WAS MIXED... PURE VAMPIRE BLOOD, UNDILUTED. WORSE THAN A BITE.
MUCH WORSE.
blugh.
EVIDENCE 684
AND I'LL TELL Y'THIS: WHOEVER GAVE HIM THAT HIT WANTED TO CAUSE A PANIC IN THIS CLUB. NO "ACCIDENT" ABOUT IT.
mrr.
HALF-FORMED MEMORY.
OUTTA MY HANDS NOW, THOUGH.
LISTEN, KID... DON'T GET Y'SELF ALL WORKED UP IN KNOTS OVER THIS THING, HUH? AIN'T YOUR FAULT THAT FREAK GOOFED HISSELF UP.
SICKOS LIKE THAT GOT ONE FOOT IN THE GRAVE AS IT IS. NOTHIN' YOU COULDA DONE.
AND SSI STARTS GIVIN' YOU TOO MUCH SHIT ON THIS, YOU JUST GIMME A HOLLER.
...ssi can kiss my ay ess ess.
...THEY'LL COME TO YOUR HOUSE, SERA.
they tried that once before, remember?
::SIGH::
328 bullet holes in the walls, lois. i counted.
ALL RIGHT, ALL RIGHT. YOU DO WHAT YOU WANT. NOT LIKE I CAN STOP YOU, ANYHOW.
oh i don't mean to–
YEAH, SURE. TELL Y'WHAT, WHY DONCHA GO HOME AND GET SOME SLEEP...
...I FIGURE YOU AND I ARE IN FOR A BUMPY PATCH A DAYS...

SERENITY ROSE (Slave Labor Graphics)

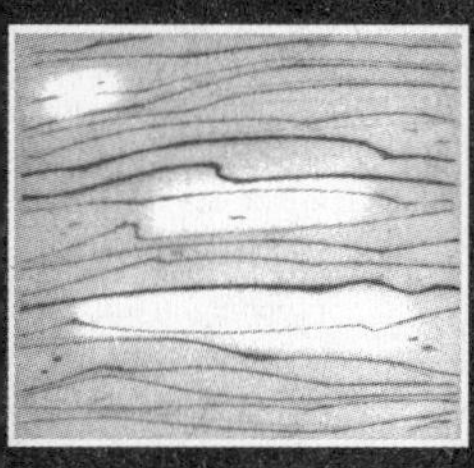
REPORTS COMING IN
VAMP ATTACK!
CHAOS IN CRESTFALLEN

LIVE
the dArkROOM
KORC-9
POLICE CALLED TO THIS LATE-NIGHT DANCE CLUB

NNN
SO-CALLED "GOTHIC" UNDERGROUND

ICBM
DETAILS SKETCHY AT THE MOMENT

AH'M FAN-GEE TH' DRACUKEY!
APPARENT VAMPIRE ATTACK

FILE
ABN
23-YEAR-OLD MICHAEL STATTEN

OVERDOSE

LIVE
VICTIM'S MOTHER
"THAT BOY... I ALWAYS KNOWED..."

eyewitness
"8-FOOT BLEEPING PONY..."

12:01
FANGS OVER CRESTFALLEN
CHASE
WE'RE NOW READY TO

witch
CONFIRMING THE INVOLVEMENT OF MS. SERENITY ELIZABETH ROSE

FILE
NBS
PERHAPS BEST KNOWN FOR HIJACKING A SCHOOL BUS AT THE AGE OF

SSI
SINGLE-HANDEDLY TOOK ON A WHOLE PLATOON OF SSI SHOCK TROOPS-

NEVER LIVED IT D-

CROSSLINE
BUT JUST WHAT WAS HER ROLE IN THIS, THIS...

DANGEROUS

SATANIC

BOX NEWS
TERRORIST

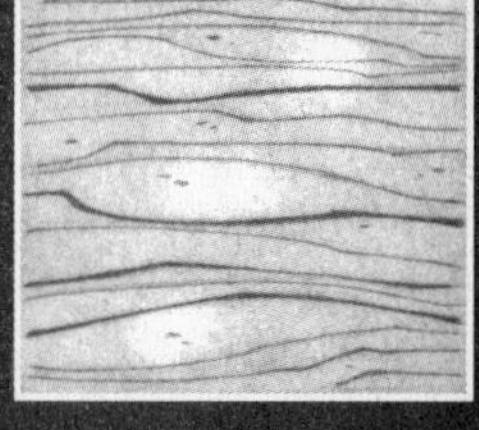
MONSTER

SERENITY ROSE (Slave Labor Graphics)

HAYULL FAHURR!

BORN FROM IT, LIVING WITH IT, **LUST**ING FOR IT, DYING IN ITS UN**HOLY** EMBRACE. THAT IS THE WAY OF THE WITCH, MR. HARDWELL. A PESTILENCE UPON OUR GOOD EARTH.

...YEAH, BUT WE'RE TALKING **VAMPIRES** HERE, DOC, NOT WITCH--

REVEREND DR. LESTER TEMPEN
CHURCH OF RIGHT THINKING

THE WITCH GAVE BIRTH TO THE VAMPIRE, SIR! IT IS **MOTHER** TO THIS **LUST**-FUL ARMY OF DREAD, BURNING WITH A NEED FOR **DEATH**. FOR **FLESH**. FOR **BLOOD**.

...AND DO YOU KNOW WHOSE BLOOD IT HUNGERS FOR THE **MOST**, MR. **HARDWELL**?

AH, THE DATA WE HAVE INDICATES VAMPIRES DON'T REALLY-

THE **BLOOD OF THE FLOCK**, MR. HARDWELL. THE FLESH OF GOD'S CHOSEN FEW.

tess!!

the hell are you watching down there?

"BARE KNUCKLES WITH CHUCK ST. HARDWELL!" YOUR **FAVORITE!** THEY'S TALKIN' 'BOUT YEEEEEWWWWW!

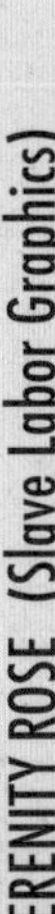
SERENITY ROSE (Slave Labor Graphics)

AW, BUT YOU'RE TALKIN' ANCIENT HISTORY HERE, DOC! THIS AIN'T GOT NOTHIN' TO DO WITH WITCHES ANYMORE. THIS "CURSE", IT'S COMIN' IN FROM CENTRAL AMERICA NOW, NOT MEDIEVAL EUROPE!
god-dammit.
OUR HOLY WAR MUST BEGIN AT THE SOURCE, SIR!
IT'S ALL THESE BANANA REPUBLICS GONE WILD, NOT A BUNCH OF WAR-LOCKS HIDING IN CASTLES!
why do they keep putting this fat man on my tv?
HRM?
this horrifying caricature of an evangelist. why does he keep showing up all the damn time?
LOUD = PROFIT.
oh yeah.
...
is that my bla-tess, why are you not in your own home right now?
what time is it?
I DUNNO... 4 PM?
OH MAN IT'S INSANE OUT THERE RIGHT NOW.. WE COULDN'T EVEN GET PAST THE GATE ON ACCOUNT OF ALL THEM REPORTERS AN' SUCH. THE WHOLE TOWN'S SWARMIN' WITH 'EM.
uuurgh... just for one stupid little vampire thing...
YEAH.
OH YEAH, AND SOMETHING ABOUT THIS INFAMOUS LITTLE WITCH WHO HASN'T BEEN HEARD FROM IN, LIKE, 6 YEARS.
MAYBE YOU'VE HEARD OF HER. SERENITY SOMTHING-OR-OTHER. STUPID NAME.

SERENITY ROSE (Slave Labor Graphics)

no, i'm not familiar.
zoe mirolette
proprietor, the mended wing inn of crestfallen.
OH, SHE SAID TO GIVE YOU A BIG HUG FROM HER...
...BUT OF COURSE I'M NOT GONNA DO ANY OF THAT SHIT.
thanks.
...so you were here all morning, then? is zoe around?
NAH, SHE'S DOWN AT THE INN. SOMETHING ABOUT THE GUESTS BEING MOBBED.
YOU HONESTLY DIDN'T KNOW WE WERE HERE?
nope.
wait... "we"?
AWWW... POOR LIL DORK IS SO ADORABLE WHEN HE SLEEPS.
MRPH...
BOO-BIES...
oh great. now a boy has seen me completely sockless...
GO GIVE HIM THE BIG HUG, WILLYA?
...he slept with his backpack on?
ZORT!
...THESE WITCHES... THEY ARE NOT LIKE YOU OR I, MR. HARDWELL...
bluuur...

THEY ARE NOT, IN FACT, HUMAN BEINGS AT ALL.
AT LEAST NOT AS WE UNDER-STAND "HUMAN."
THE FLESH OF THE WITCH... IS MADE FROM BLACKEST SHADOW. ITS HANDS FROM BURNING SIN.
ITS HATEFUL MIND, A PUTRID CANCER TORN FROM THE FESTERING SIDE OF SATAN HIMSELF.
AND ITS HEART...
ITS HEART FORGED FROM THE SEARED REMAINS OF A THOUSAND UNBORN BABES.
NO, THESE ARE NOT HUMANS, MR. HARDWELL.
THESE ARE DEMONS MOST FOUL, SET UPON THE EARTH TO BEDEVIL ALL THE PEOPLES OF THE WORLD, TO LEAD MAN TO RUINATION...
AND TO TEST THE COURAGE OF THE CHOSEN.
"...WELL, THANK YOU FOR KEEPING THE HYPERBOLE TO A MINIMUM, DOCTOR."

SERENITY ROSE (Slave Labor Graphics)

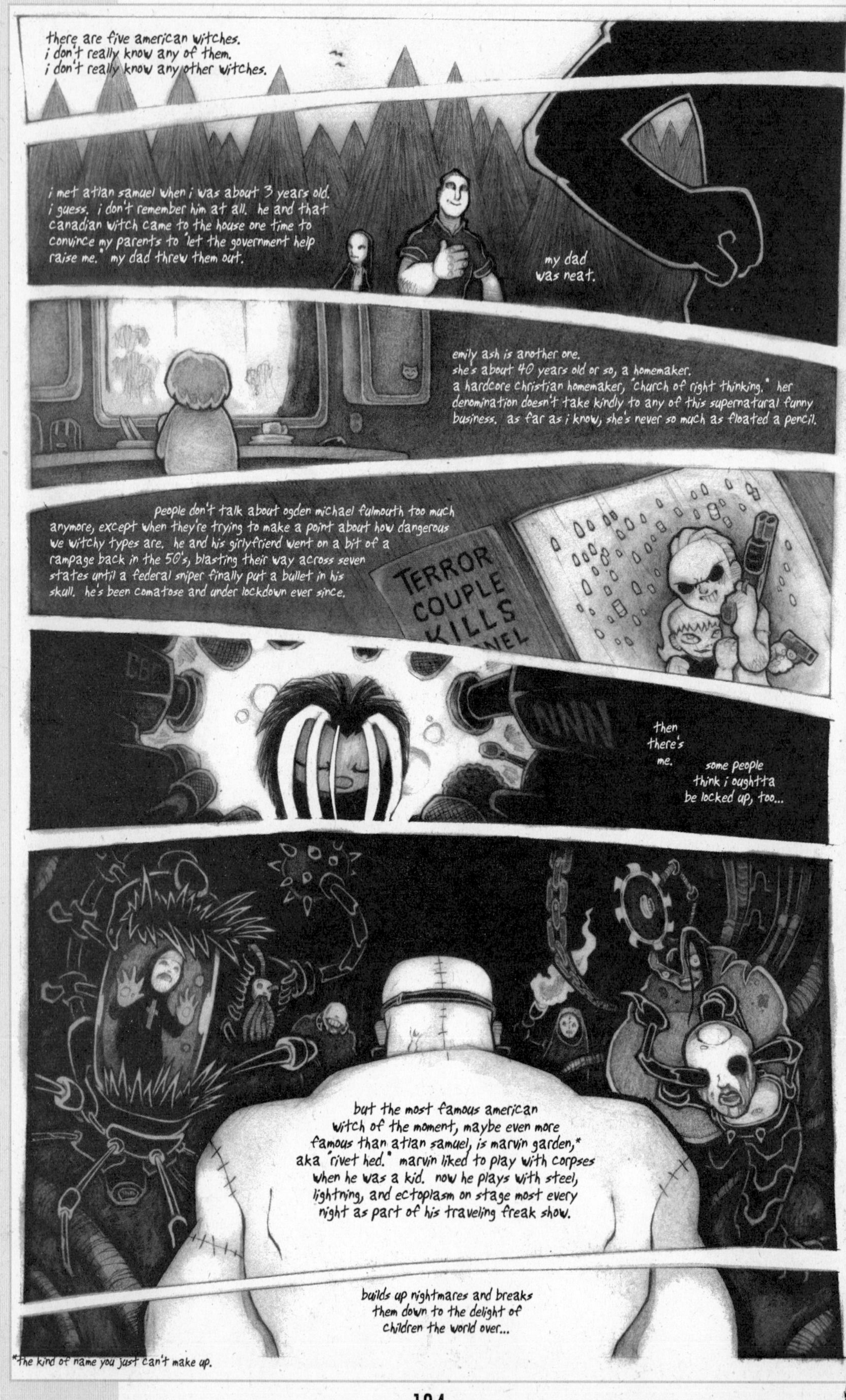

there are five american witches.
i don't really know any of them.
i don't really know any other witches.

i met atlan samuel when i was about 3 years old. i guess. i don't remember him at all. he and that canadian witch came to the house one time to convince my parents to "let the government help raise me." my dad threw them out.

my dad was neat.

emily ash is another one.
she's about 40 years old or so, a homemaker.
a hardcore christian homemaker, "church of right thinking." her denomination doesn't take kindly to any of this supernatural funny business. as far as i know, she's never so much as floated a pencil.

people don't talk about ogden michael fulmouth too much anymore, except when they're trying to make a point about how dangerous we witchy types are. he and his girlyfriend went on a bit of a rampage back in the 50's, blasting their way across seven states until a federal sniper finally put a bullet in his skull. he's been comatose and under lockdown ever since.

TERROR COUPLE KILLS ...NEL

then there's me.

some people think i oughtta be locked up, too...

but the most famous american witch of the moment, maybe even more famous than atlan samuel, is marvin garden,* aka "rivet hed." marvin liked to play with corpses when he was a kid. now he plays with steel, lightning, and ectoplasm on stage most every night as part of his traveling freak show.

builds up nightmares and breaks them down to the delight of children the world over...

*the kind of name you just can't make up.

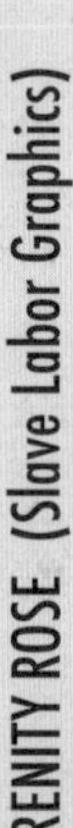

TCHHHHHHHSH
HE'S LOOSE!
I'LL KILL ALL OF YOU!
SKRAK
NNGNNN!
JEPH LOEB JIM LEE S. WILLIAMS
IN THE MOUTH OF MADNESS!
BATMAN
I need to know **who** orchestrated the kidnapping...
BDOK
NO.
YOU WON'T HURT ANYONE ELSE.
...taught my enemy new methods...
SLAM
TOO SLOW.
...and what happened to the money.

I made a promise on the grave of my parents to rid this city of the evil that took their lives. By day, I am Bruce Wayne, billionaire philanthropist. At night, criminals, a cowardly and superstitious lot, call me...

BATMAN CREATED BY BOB KANE

HUSH

Chapter Three THE BEAST

Leaving me
to send a monster
to catch a monster.

KRASH
I'M GETTING OUTTA HERE. GET MY MONEY BACK.
ALL UNITS! GET SOME HELP DOWN HERE!

GO AHEAD. FOLLOW ME.
I HAVEN'T EATEN SINCE LUNCH.
TRECHHH

I DON'T LIKE THIS.
I DON'T LIKE *YOU*.
No one seriously injured. The guards will get double hazard pay. And Croc has escaped.
So far, so good.

BATMAN (DC Comics)

THAT'S ALL RIGHT. I'M NOT HERE TO BE LIKED.
I DON'T NEED TO REMIND YOU THAT THE FATHER OF THE BOY THAT... BEAST...KIDNAPPED IS A PERSONAL FRIEND OF THE PRESIDENT.
Amanda Waller heads up President Luthor's Office of Meta-Human Affairs.
I have history with Waller. None of it pleasant.
That's all right. I'm not here to be liked either.

Dealing with anything remotely connected to Luthor makes my skin crawl. But, Croc was about to be transferred out of my city...
YOU MEAN HE'S A MAJOR CONTRIBUTOR TO LUTHOR'S CAMPAIGN PARTY.
YOU'VE GOT UNTIL MIDNIGHT.
THEN, CROC IS OURS.

KRAKA THOOM
MASTER BRUCE...?
GO AHEAD, ALFRED.
A CAR JUST PULLED UP TO THE HOUSE. ARE WE EXPECTING COMPANY?
NO.
PHILADELPHIA LICENSE PLATE. HMX 19...I CAN'T MAKE OUT THE LAST NUMBER IN THIS STORM.
I have until midnight...

Life through whispers
by Xaime
2004

WENT TO THE MOVIES THE OTHER NIGHT WITH JOE FROM WORK AND HIS COUSIN LOUIE FROM BELL GARDENS. CRACKING ME UP WITH THEIR USUAL BICKERING AND SPECIAL BRAND OF CHICANO UNHUMOR.
THE INCREDIBLE
SHRINKING MAN

AFTER THE MOVIE THE GUYS WEREN'T READY TO HEAD HOME JUST YET SO WE POPPED INTO CHEETAH TORPEDA'S FOR A NIGHTCAP AND A LITTLE POOCHIE.

I HADN'T BEEN THERE FOR SOME TIME, EVER SINCE MY FAVORITE DANCER AND OVERALL HEARTBREAKER, THE LOVELY VELVET, OR VIVIAN I GUESS IS HER REAL NAME, DISAPPEARED. JUST WHEN I GOT TO KNOW
LOVE AND ROCKETS
NO. 10

COME TO THINK OF IT, I HADN'T SEEN ANYBODY IN SOME TIME. EVER SINCE DOYLE CAME OUT AND TRIED TO GIVE ME THAT HUMMER WHEN WE WERE BOTH SCHNOCKERED, THINGS SLOWED DOWN QUITE A BIT. MAYBE HE'S EMBARRASSED ABOUT IT, I DUNNO, MAYBE IT'S ME.

THEN LIKE A LARK, THIS ONE BLONDE WHO SITS DOWN WITH US TURNS OUT TO BE ONE OF DOYLE'S GANG FROM THAT DIVE ON LAS PALMAS AND ASKS ME WHY I'M NOT OVER THERE WITH EVERYBODY CELEBRATING ITS LAST NIGHT OPEN.
1

ALL I KNOW IS 'EVERYBODY' BETTER MEAN VIVIAN SO I ASK THE GUYS IF THEY WANT TO HIT IT UP BUT THEY'RE TOO BUSY HITTING THE BLONDE UP FOR LAP DANCES SO I LEFT WITHOUT THEIR SORRY ASSES.
EXI

SO, WAS SHE GONNA REMEMBER ME? I MEAN, WE ONLY TALKED ONCE. AND WHAT IF SHE'S WITH THAT SLIMY MOBSTER GUY SID? WHAT IF SHE'S NOT EVEN THERE?? WHAT IF...? SHIT, I'M TOO OLD FOR THIS.

TOO OLD TO BE HOPPING AROUND TOWN IN PURSUIT OF A PRETTY GIRL. TOO OLD TO BE WASTING TIME NOT BEING IN PURSUIT OF THIS PRETTY GIRL. TOO OLD PERIOD. THEN AGAIN, WHAT ELSE SHOULD I BE WASTING MY TIME ON?

SO THE PLACE IS PACKED. I DON'T SEE DOYLE OR VIVIAN BUT THERE'S THAT CRAZY SILENT FUCKER, THE ONE THEY CALL BORNEO, BEATING THE HOLY SHIT OUT OF SOME POOR BASTARD. I CAN SEE THE FUN HAS ALREADY STARTED.

TEN MINUTES AND I HAD IT. VIV OR NO VIV, I DECIDED TO JET BEFORE I RAN INTO MY OWN BULLSHIT. SO THEN, I'M NOT TWO FEET FROM THE EXIT AND BLAM! THERE IT IS. MY HEART JOLTED BUT I STILL MANAGED TO MAKE IT OUTSIDE.

DAMN, WAS IT REALLY HER? WAS IT MAGGIE? MAGGIE WITH DIFFERENT HAIR? WHAT THE HELL WAS SHE DOING HERE? WELL, I KNOW SHE KNOWS DOYLE, BUT... DOES SHE KNOW VIVIAN, TOO? FUCK, DID SHE NOTICE ME? SHE LOOKED RIGHT AT ME! MY GOD, WHAT'S NEXT?
2

LOVE AND ROCKETS (Fantagraphics)

I'LL TELL YOU WHAT'S NEXT. VIVACIOUS VIV AND SLIMY SID, THAT'S WHAT. THEY SEEMED TO BE IN PRIVATE CONVERSATION. BEFORE I COULD SLIP BACK INTO THE BAR, THEY SPOTTED ME AND VIVIAN SAID HI.

I SAID HI BACK BUT BEFORE I COULD ESCAPE SHE CALLED ME OVER IN THAT FOGHORN VOICE OF HERS. ON ANY OTHER OCCASION IT WOULD BE HEAVEN BUT AT THIS MOMENT I WANTED TO GO HOME AND HIDE UNDER MY BED.

SHE ASKED ME HOW I'D BEEN LIKE WE WERE OLD PALS. I COULDN'T TELL, WAS I SAVING HER FROM THAT SLIME WHO JUST KEPT GLARING AT ME LIKE HE WAS STUDYING MY FACE SO HE'D KNOW WHO TO HAVE KILLED LATER?

HATE TO ADMIT IT, BUT AS MUCH AS I'D LOVE TO BE HER KNIGHT IN SHINING ARMOR, I WANTED TO GET THE HELL OUT OF THERE MUCH MORE. I TOLD HER I HAD TO PEE BUT THAT I'D SEE HER INSIDE. PURDY SMOOVE, EH?

THEN I MADE MY SMOOVE EXIT (WHICH WAS MORE LIKE A FAST MOTION SCENE FROM GILLIGAN'S ISLAND) BUT I WENT IN THE WRONG DIRECTION AND ENDED UP RIGHT AROUND THE CORNER DEAD ENDED IN A FLOWER BED.

I DIDN'T DARE MOVE, HOPING THEY WOULD THINK I TOOK OFF DOWN THE STREET. I COULD STILL HEAR THEIR VOICES BUT COULDN'T MAKE OUT THEIR CONVERSATION. I THINK THEY WERE ARGUING ABOUT FOLK ART.
3

THERE I WAS, TRAPPED IN THIS STUPID, FUCKING SITUATION WHEN I COULD HAVE BEEN SITTING WITH BORING OL' JOE FROM WORK AND HIS COUSIN LOUIE WITH THEIR CRUMMY JOKES WATCHING POOCHIE.

THEN I THOUGHT ABOUT SEEING MAGGIE. I HADN'T SEEN HER IN SO LONG. GOD, SHE WAS BEAUTIFUL. SHE'S LIKE, THIS WOMAN NOW. THIS... JUST WHEN YOU THINK YOU GOT IT ALL FIGURED OUT... MAN O MAN.

BUT THEN I STARTED THINKING ABOUT HOW WE SHOULD HAVE NEVER BROKE UP AND ALL THAT SHIT BUT BEFORE I COULD BLAME THE WHOLE WORLD FOR MY BITTERNESS, I HEARD SOME RUDE SOUNDS AROUND THE CORNER.

I SWORE SID WAS HURTING VIVIAN BUT WHEN I DARTED OUT TO TRY AND STOP IT THEY WERE NOT THERE. BUT FURTHER DOWN THE WAY WAS DOYLE. HE WAS WATCHING SOMETHING GOING ON IN THE PARKING LOT.

IT LOOKED LIKE THE GUY BORNEO AND ANOTHER GUY WERE HELPING SOMEONE INTO A CAR. BUT BEFORE I COULD SEE MORE, DOYLE BLOCKED MY VIEW AND ASKED ME WHERE THE FUCK MY SAGGY ASS HAS BEEN.

I ASKED HIM WHAT WAS UP AND HE SAID SOME ASSBITE GOT TOO DRUNK AND THEY WERE TAKING HIM HOME. I GET IT, FIRST, BLOODY UP THE GUY AND THEN NURSE HIS WOUNDS. THEN, DOYLE TOOK ME IN TO BUY ME A DRINK AND ASKED IF I'D SEEN VIVIAN YET.
4

LOVE AND ROCKETS (Fantagraphics)

SHE WAS SITTING INSIDE BY HERSELF. I ASKED DOYLE IF THAT SID FUCK WAS STILL AROUND AND HE JUST LAUGHED AND SAID, "THE FUCKER'S MARRIED." I'M NOT SURE WHAT THAT MEANT BUT I FELT A LITTLE EASIER TO SIT WITH HER.

THERE SHE WAS, STICKIN' STICKIN' STICKIN' BUT NOW SHE WASN'T TALKING. DOYLE SAID HE'D GO GET MY DRINK AND THEN SHOT ME THAT 'GO FOR IT' GLANCE BEFORE HE LEFT. JUST LIKE THE FUCKER USED TO DO IN HIGH SCHOOL.

SHE AND I SAT THERE FOR AWHILE NOT TALKING. THEN JUST WHEN I WAS ABOUT TO ASK HER IF SHE KNEW MAGGIE, SHE DECIDED TO SPEAK. FROGMOUTHLIKE, SHE ASKED ME WHY I WEAR A SUIT.

I DECIDED TO BE CHARMING AND USE AN OLD STANDBY. I SAID THAT EVERY ONCE IN AWHILE A MAN OUGHT TO WEAR A SUIT. IT WENT NOWHERE. SHEESH, IMAGINE IF SHE KNEW THE JACKET AND PANTS DIDN'T EVEN MATCH.

THEN DOYLE CAME BACK AND RIGHT AWAY HE ASKED ME IF I COULD TAKE VIVIAN HOME LATER. I SHRUGGED, THEN HE GAVE HER THE 'BEHAVE YOURSELF' LOOK. I STARTED TO FEEL LIKE I WAS BEING SET UP, BUT NOT FOR A DATE.

THE NEXT HALF HOUR I SPENT IN THAT BAR WAS JUST PLAIN WEIRD. PEOPLE COMING IN AND OUT. A LOT OF WHISPERING BACK AND FORTH. AND WHERE DID MAGGIE GO? I NEED SOMEONE NORMAL AROUND.

THEN IT WAS TIME TO GO. DOYLE WALKED OUT WITH US. HE TOLD ME I WAS A GALLANT KNIGHT FOR DRIVING VIVIAN HOME. I TOLD HIM TO SUCK MY DICK. THEN I SAID, NEVER MIND. THINGS GOT NORMAL FOR A SECOND.

THEN I SAW THE GUY, OR I THINK IT WAS THE GUY THAT BORNEO BEAT THE FUCK OUT OF. DID HE COME BACK FOR MORE? HE REALLY DIDN'T SEEM THAT DRUNK. I DUNNO, IT GOT REAL STRANGE ALL OVER AGAIN.

THEN I SAW IT. THE PUDDLE OF BLOOD IN THE PARKING LOT AND SOMETHING CLICKED IN MY HEAD AND I GOT A COLD CHILL. THEN I SWEAR I HEARD DOYLE SAY UNDER HIS BREATH, "THOSE FUCKERS WENT AND DID IT."

I LOOKED AT HIM AND HE HAD THE SADDEST LOOK ON HIS FACE, THEN IT CHANGED AS HE LOOKED AT ME LIKE WE BOTH KNEW SOMETHING, THEN HE SAID TO MAKE SURE VIV GETS HOME OK AND THEN HE WAS GONE.

AS I DROVE VIVIAN HOME SHE STARTED TO OPEN UP. SHE ASKED ME IF I KNEW A GIRL NAMED MAGGIE. I DON'T KNOW WHY BUT I JUST SAID "YEAH, THROUGH DOYLE." SHE SIGHED AND SAID, "EVERYTHING'S THROUGH DOYLE."

BUT I WASN'T REALLY LISTENING. ALL I COULD DO WAS PICTURE SOMEONE'S FUCKED UP DEAD BODY LAYING SOMEWHERE IN THE L.A. RIVER. THEN I WONDERED WHERE JOE AND LOUIE WERE, CRUMMY JOKES AND ALL.
THE END

<Hi, mom?>
<How are you?>

<Yeah, I'm putting your money to good use, see?>

CLICK!

LA PERDIDA
PART FOUR BY JESSICA ABEL

¡Oscar!

¡Hola, mi amor!
Carlita.

LA PERDIDA (Fantagraphics)

What's up? What have you been doing?
I'm going out. I just came to pick up some stuff. I'll be back later.

I haven't seen you in days! Where are you going? Can I go?
Can you—
No, I gotta... I'm meeting José Maria. And Ricardo

You going to a cantina? I'm so bored!
Look, I gotta hurry.

You doing some big deal? What's going on? What's Ricardo doing to you?

You've gotta get out of this stuff, Oscar!

You're gonna get in trouble...
Bye!

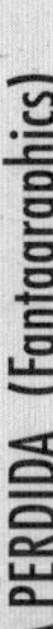
LA PERDIDA (Fantagraphics)

¡OSCAR!

<Fuck.>

<Oscar, what are you up to?>

<Oh my god! I've got to water the plant!>

"Police and legal authorities responded to accusations by the American Embassy by..." hm...

"...pointing out that they have located two of the buildings in which Powell was kept, just days after he was..."
<God it's cold.> brrrrr...
<Fucking Oscar.>
<Asshole.>
<... can't treat me like just a roommate...>

LA PERDIDA (Fantagraphics)

THE DEMON INVASION HAS BEGUN!
MY BONES ARE STAINED WITH THE BLOOD OF THE DAMNED.
I NOTICED. STAY OFF THE SOFA.
DEMON INVASION!
YAHOOEY!
COME ON! I GOTTA GO!
I'LL BE OUT IN A MINUTE!
HEY! WHO ATE THE LAST ZINGER?!
HEE HEE HEE!
GUESS WHO I POSSESSED! BLARG!
HEY! GET OUT OF THERE!
I'M GETTING THE SQUIRT GUN!
GRARR
GNARR GRARR
CLICK!
HEY, WAS THAT YOUR FOOT?
SORRY, MAN, SERIOUSLY, GO BACK TO SLEEP
WHATCHA WORKIN' ON? CAN I SEE? HUH? CAN I SEE? CAN I HELP? LEMME SEE!
GRR_
HSU AND CHAN

HSU AND CHAN (Slave Labor Graphics)

BY ALL THAT'S HOLY--
THIS MUST STOP!

CHAN! CHAN! LOOK... AT... THIS!

IT... UM... IT LOOKS LIKE A TOOTHBRUSH.
IT'S MY TOOTHBRUSH!

...IT LOOKS FINE.
TAKE A WHIFF.

SHORTLY...
WE'VE FACED HORRORS IN OUR LIVES BEFORE-- DEATHS IN THE FAMILY, AWKWARD DATING SITUATIONS, "ERIN BROCKAVICH," UNSIGHTLY RASHES, A TRIP TO FRANCE--
BUT THIS... THIS NIGHTMARE OF DEMONIC SHENANIGANS MUST BE BROUGHT TO A HALT!
MY NOSTRILS.. BURNING.. :GACK!:
BY ALL THE VARIED AND OFTEN INEFFECTUAL FORCES OF GOODNESS AND LIGHT IN THIS WORLD, WE MUST WAGE A WAR ON HELL ITSELF!
OR, AT LEAST, THE REPRESENTATIVES THEREOF WHICH ARE CURRENTLY SULPHURING UP THE LIVING ROOM!
TO ARMS!

WH-- WHAT ARE WE GOING TO DO?
WE'RE GOING TO DESTROY THE FORCES OF EVIL.

OKAY, I SUPPOSE I SORT OF MEANT, "HOW ARE WE GOING TO DO THIS?"
OH.
I DUNNO, HIT THEM WITH STUFF, I GUESS.
WE DID GET THOSE RUBBER MALLETS A WHILE AGO, AND NEVER GOT A CHANCE TO USE 'EM...

DON'T YOU THINK WE MIGHT WANT TO FIND SOME WEAPONS THAT ARE A BIT MORE... SPIRITUAL IN NATURE?
OH, SURE, CHAN -- LET'S JUST HOLD A SEANCE AND SEE IF WE CAN'T SUMMON THE ETERNAL SOUL OF A BLACKJACK OR SOMETHING, VERY INTELLIGENT.
NOW COME HELP ME LOOK FOR THE BB RIFLE.

I MEAN THE BOOK, HSU! IF IT BROUGHT THEM HERE, MAYBE IT CAN GET RID OF THEM, TOO!
HMM... WELL, WE'LL HAVE TO HIT 'EM WITH IT PRETTY HARD...

HSU AND CHAN (Slave Labor Graphics)

SOME WHERE IN THIS BOOK THERE HAS TO BE A PASSAGE OR INCANTATION OR SOMETHING THAT WE CAN USE TO SEND THESE CREATURES BACK TO HELL!
OH, SURE, IT WORKED OUT SWELL FOR THE LAST GUY.

WHATCHA GUYS READIN'?
NONE OF YOUR BEESWAX.
OKAY, HERE'S ONE THAT'LL SUMMON MORE DEMONS, THIS ONE WILL SUMMON A SPECIAL KIND OF DEMON, HERE IT LOOKS LIKE THE GUY JUST NEEDED SOME SCRATCH PAPER, BECAUSE IT'S A RECIPE FOR OLIVE LOAF...

I SUPPOSE THIS IS GONNA TAKE A WHILE, RIGHT?
I'M GONNA GO GRAB A SANDWICH.
NO WORRIES, CHIEF, I GOT YOU COVERED!
RECITATIONS TO KEEP A SPIRIT EARTHBOUND, SOMETHING ABOUT A HALF-MAN/ HALF-TOAD PROJECT...

IS THERE AN INDEX?
WHAT? NO, OF COURSE THERE'S NO IND--
WAIT, YES THERE IS, I'LL BE DARNED. "DEMON REMOVAL," PAGE 70.

HA HA!
HUSH... "SPIRITS SUMMONED CAN ONLY BE REMOVED BY TOTAL EXORCISM, A FEAT OUTSIDE THE SCOPE OF THIS EXPERIMENT"-- DRAT! --"THE SPIRITS CAN, HOWEVER, BE IMPRISONED WITHIN OBJECTS OF HUMAN CONSTRUCTION AND CONTAINED INDEFINITELY, BY USE OF THE FOLLOWING SYMBOLS..."

HERE, TAKE THESE DOWN-- THIS ONE LOOKS LIKE A HALF-MOON SHAPE, SORTA, WITH AN EYEBALL PEERING OUT FROM THE CENTER...
RIGHT, RIGHT...

EEP!
POOF!
SHLURP!

PLINK!

OH, YOU BUM.
HOT DOG!

HEY, I'M BACK. I MISS ANYTHING?
YOU BET YOU DID! WATCH THIS!
'MMM, DELICIOUS OREO COOKIES!'
WHERE?

AHA!
YIKES!
POOF!

HUH?
SHOOP

SHLURP!

I GUESS ANY GIVEN OBJECT CAN ONLY HANDLE ONE DEMON.

HUH.

I'M NOT GOING TO EAT THIS, NOW.

WHAT'S ON HERE?

MUENSTER?

HSU AND CHAN (Slave Labor Graphics)

WELL, WE KNOW HOW TO TAKE CARE OF OUR DEMON PROBLEM, NOW!
LET'S CLEAN HOUSE!
HANG ON.. EACH OBJECT WE USE CAN ONLY HOLD ONE SPIRIT..
THERE ARE HUNDREDS OF THEM OUT THERE!
WHERE WOULD WE BE ABLE TO FIND OVER A HUNDRED RANDOM...
...
SOON...
HISSS
ALRIGHT, MINIONS OF DARKNESS.. IT'S TIME TO SAY GOODNIGHT...
... COURTESY OF GRAN'MA TANAKA'S KNICK-KNACK CABINET!
EAT QUAINT PORCELAIN FARMER FIGURINE, HELLSPAWN!
ZOIKS!
THE BATTLE RAGES FOR A REASONABLE LENGTH OF TIME...
POOF!
NOOOOOOOOO!
LET'S SEE YOU DO ANY MORE EVIL INSIDE A SET OF NOVELTY SALT AND PEPPER SHAKERS SHAPED LIKE DUCKS!
HEY, I'M ONLY SLIGHTLY LESS HORRIFYING, NOW!
SHLURP!
EEK!
WISCONSIN
POP!
SO, YOU HAVE CHOSEN TO BETRAY US!
YOU WILL SUFFER THE CONSEQUENCES OF YOUR ACTIONS!
YOU WILL BEG FOR DEATH FAR BEFORE IT IS GRANTED!
A RIVER OF BLOOD SHALL FLOW FROM THIS HOUSE!
I WILL TEAR YOUR BODIES APART!
YOUR FLESH WILL BE--
BE...
OH, DRAT.
COOKI
MAKE SURE THAT JAR GETS MARKED.
IS THAT ALL OF THEM?

HSU AND CHAN (Slave Labor Graphics)

I THINK SO..
GOOD THING, TOO-- WE'RE DOWN TO THE TOOTHPICK HOLDER FROM HAWAII AND THE NAPKIN DISPENSER IN THE SHAPE OF A TURTLE.
WELL, I TRUST WE'VE LEARNED A VALUABLE LESSON FROM THIS WHOLE FIASCO?
HELP! I FEEL PRECIOUS!

OH, ASSUREDLY, BROTHER CHAN-- THIS EXPERIENCE HAS OPENED MY EYES TO THE POSSIBILITY THAT SOME KNOWLEDGE, HOWEVER ATTRACTIVE OR DRIPPING WITH TV MOVIE POTENTIAL IT MAY BE, SIMPLY WAS NEVER MEANT TO FALL INTO THE HANDS OF --
WHEW, IT SURE GOT HOT IN HERE ALL OF A SUDDEN...

CRIPES!
AHK'TULA--
--MA--
AHK--
ACH?
THAT ONE THING!
IT'S HERE!
BOOM!

YEAH, NOBODY SAW THAT COMING. BIG SURPRISE, ROD SERLING.
CHAN!
LOOK OUT!

HSU AND CHAN (Slave Labor Graphics)

EEP!
GRAB!

AAAA..
HEY! THE HENDERSONS GOT A LAWN FOUNTAIN!
AAAAIIGH!
STAY THERE, CHAN!
I'LL SAVE YOU!

TSK! THOSE STEVENSONS, WILL THEY EVER MOW THEIR LAWN?
HEY! OVER HERE!
THIS WAY, OCTO-WUSS!

I DON'T KNOW HOW THEY DO THINGS WHERE YOU COME FROM, BUT AROUND HERE, WHEN WE WANT TO DEVOUR SOMEONE'S SOUL-- WHICH WE DON'T, VERY OFTEN-- WE ASK PERMISSION, FIRST!
IT'S TIME FOR ME TO TEACH YOU SOME MANNERS!

GREETINGS FROM HAWAII, SUCKER!

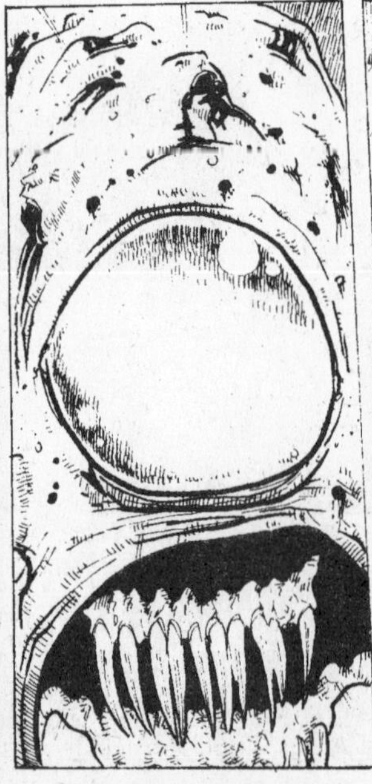

WITH THIS OFFICIALLY-LICENSED PRODUCT OF THE HAWAIIAN ISLANDS ..
ZING!
-- I SEND YOU BACK TO DARKNESS!

HSU AND CHAN (Slave Labor Graphics)

KA-
BONK!

MELE-
KALIKIMAKA IS A THING WE SAY..

GREAT SCOTT! IT'S TOO STRONG TO BE CAPTURED!
DIFFERENT TACTIC, HSU-- TRY HITTING IT WITH STUFF!
BUT DON'T LET IT CATCH YOU, OR IT'S ALL OVER!

OH -- UM, RIGHT, I'M WORKING ON IT --
CRIKEY, CAN'T YOU TAKE A JOKE?

AAAAIGH!
WOW, THAT'S A UNIQUE SMELL!
CHAN!
CHAN--

H-HOLD-- MY.. MAIL!

OH, WAY TO GO.

HSU AND CHAN (Slave Labor Graphics)

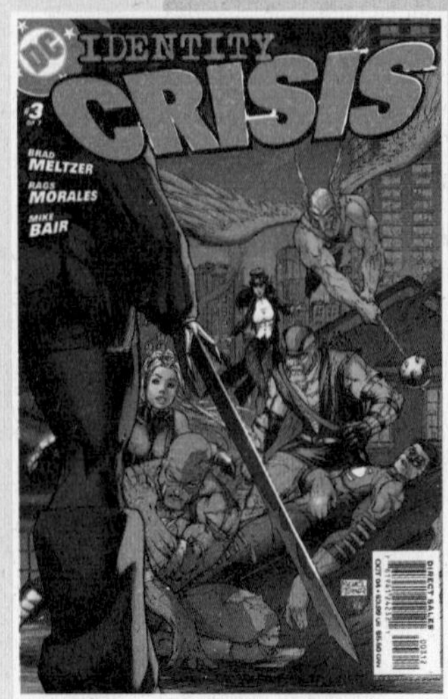
DC
IDENTITY CRISIS
#3
BRAD MELTZER
RAGS MORALES
MIKE BAIR

OPTIC NERVE
9

MARVEL
ASTONISHING X-MEN

KIRKMAN • OTTLEY • CRABTREE
INVINCIBLE
PERFECT STRANGERS
Introduction by Tom Brevoort

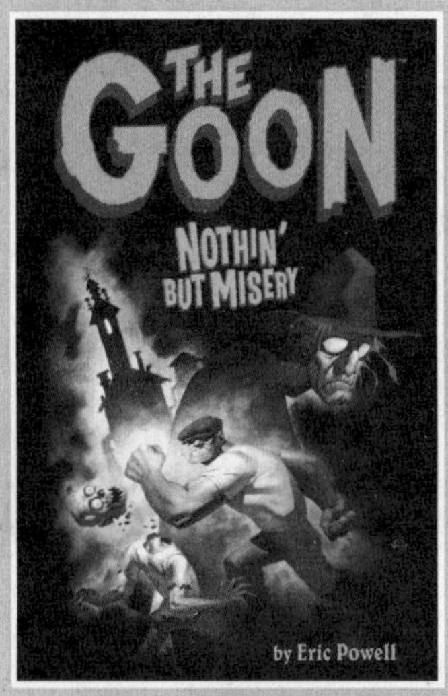
THE GOON
NOTHIN' BUT MISERY
by Eric Powell

ROBERT KIRKMAN CHARLIE ADLARD CLIFF RATHBURN
THE WALKING DEAD
VOLUME 3
SAFETY BEHIND BARS

FINDER
THE RESCUERS
LIGHT SPEED PRESS

small gods
Killing Grin

DOC FRANKENSTEIN

DC: THE NEW FRONTIER

DC: THE new frontier

DC: The New Frontier

THE LUNA BROTHERS
ULTRA
SEVEN DAYS

DAVID LAPHAM
STRAY BULLETS
36
EL CAPITAN

EIGHTBALL

Farewell, Georgia
FOUR FOLKTALES

Skyscrapers
1
of the Midwest

AMERICAN ELF

Manga

By Jake T. Forbes

Ever since the "manga boom" took the publishing world by storm in 2002, people have been searching for the secret to manga's success. In principle, *manga* is just the Japanese word for comics. The concept of telling stories through sequential art transcends language and nationality, and while the tools and techniques used by Japanese *manga-ka* and Western comics artists differ, both are more alike than different. The business and consumption of manga, however, is so fundamentally different from American comics as to dwarf their similarities. Manga really is ubiquitous in Japan and read by people of all ages and walks of life. It's cheap, convenient, and disposable, thanks to the "phone book" anthologies for which most manga is created. And because manga is so universally accepted in Japan, the market can support incredible diversity of subjects and styles.

The role that manga plays in Japan is much like cable television here. Instead of channels, anthologies cater to specific tastes and demographics. In addition to the high-school-romance and action-themed books, there are anthologies specializing in mystery, fantasy or horror for genre enthusiasts; "Office Lady" and "Salaryman" anthologies for white-collar workers; and there are entire magazines dedicated to just golf, pachinko (a kind of pinball-gambling), and the tile game Mah-Jongg. The collected editions, or *tankobon*, are the equivalents of DVDs in that they feature better quality printing and are books one tends to keep.

It was only when U.S. publishers stopped trying to fit manga into the failing comic book mold and adopted something closer to the Japanese system that manga really took off over here. Cheaper prices, a smaller trim size and a more "authentic" presentation—complete with right-to-left reading order—were all key to manga's triple digit growth. More important, however, was the willingness to embrace manga's diversity and publish series that didn't fit the model expected from comics.

One of the earliest success stories in American manga publishing is the work of CLAMP, the prolific four-woman studio. The group's ability to switch art styles and genres, from the baroque and apocalyptic *X/1999* to the wispy romance *Wish* won them fans of both genders and helped redefine (for better or worse) what manga looked like to the mainstream. To this day, their crossover hit *Chobits*, a bittersweet sci-fi romance, is a "gateway drug" for new manga readers.

Long the backbone of the boys manga in Japan, *Shonen Jump* is leading the way for new action titles in America. With over a half dozen series currently running on TV taken from the *Shonen Jump* imprint, as well as video games, toys, and apparel, this is manga at its most mainstream. But as the brand matures, we're starting to see less-traditional boys fare work its way in. Who would have

Table of Contents

guessed five years ago that *Hikaru no Go*, a series about a ghost teaching a boy the secrets of an ancient board game, would sell to kids in America?

Shojo (girls) manga has been the most talked about category as it opened the world's eyes to the fact that *gasp!* girls will read comics. Whereas *shonen* (boys) manga tends to focus on goal-based conflict (overcoming the external forces or personal demons necessary to win the game or beat the bad guys), shojo manga tends to be more about enduring the constant barrage of emotions that defines being a teenager. Sometimes the situations feel painfully real, other times they're wickedly excessive. Often they're both at the same time, as is the case with *Hot Gimmick*. The story of a high-school-age girl who gets blackmailed into becoming the personal slave of the cold-hearted (but cute!) boy next door keeps the emotional level turned up, yet keeps the characters sympathetic to the reader.

While it is teen-friendly fare that dominates manga sales in America, there remains a trickle of classic series that showcase the best of manga as an art form. At the top of anyone's manga reading list should be the work of Osamu Tezuka. His work has been getting new attention in translation thanks to the recent releases of *Astro Boy*, *Phoenix*, and *Buddha*. There's a reason why any manga creator you ask will list him as in influence—no one else in Japan, if not the world, understood as well as he the emotional and narrative potential of the sequential-art medium.

Manga represents a path that comics could have taken in America, if over the past few decades the format hadn't developed the stigma of being for nerdy guys and kids. Slowly but surely the comics industry is working to change perceptions. In the meantime, there's no rush—there's plenty of great content to read from Japan!

Manga

NAUSICAÄ
Of The Valley Of The Wind
2

NAUSICAÄ
Of The Valley Of The Wind
1
HAYAO MIYAZAKI

editor's choice
phoenix
DAWN
OSAMU TEZUKA
vol.1

editor's choice
phoenix
KARMA
OSAMU TEZUKA
vol.4

NARUTO
SHONEN JUMP GRAPHIC NOVEL
Story & Art by
Masashi Kishimoto volume 6

NARUTO
SHONEN JUMP GRAPHIC NOVEL
Story & Art by
Masashi Kishimoto volume 7

shôjo
IMADOKI!
Nowadays
Story and art by
Yû Watase
Volume 1

shôjo
IMADOKI!
Nowadays
Rose
Story and art by
Yû Watase
Volume 4

editor's choice
Blue Spring
BLUE SPRING™
by Taiyo Matsumoto

KENT, LET ME GO. THIS IS ALREADY HARD ENOUGH ON ME.
YOU CAN'T DO THIS TO ME. SOMETHING ABOUT YOU-- YOU'RE NOT LIKE ANYONE I'VE EVER MET.
AI!
AI, I'VE BEEN WAITING FOR YOU-- YOU REALLY HAD ME WORRIED!
And, yes, I know you didn't know I was waiting...
HM?
Princess Ai
TOKYOPOP
1
OH, NOW I SEE--YOU THINK YOU'RE HER DUPE?
GIVE IT UP!
......!!
DON'T BE A DOG WHO CHASES SPEEDING CARS...
...YOU'LL JUST GET YOURSELF RUN OVER.

THOSE WINGS ARE BEAUTIFUL...
...JUST LIKE YOU.
...THANK YOU.

THANK YOU, KENT, BUT...
...YOU HAVE TO STAY AWAY FROM ME.
AI, THIS IS WHERE YOU WORK?
LOOKS pretty High-class.
I DON'T GET WHY YOU'LL BE ANY SAFER HERE.
KENT--
WHAT?
THERE'S ONE THING I KNOW FOR SURE-- BEING AROUND ME IS VERY DANGEROUS.

YOU HAVE... WINGS...?
MY clothes are a mess...
WHAT... ARE YOU...?
THANK HEAVENS YOU'RE OKAY!
I WISH THEY'D GO AWAY...
THINGS HAVE BEEN COMING BACK TO ME-- LITTLE BY LITTLE...
...BUT THESE WINGS... I HAVE NO IDEA WHAT THEY MEAN.
EVEN I DON'T KNOW.
HUH...

--SO I'M DEFINITELY NOT YOURS!
SNAP
flap
GRAB
WINGS ...?!
A HUMAN WITH WINGS...?!
SNICKER! AND SHE DOESN'T EVEN KNOW HOW TO USE THEM...
creak
creak
CRACK
OWW!
WATER...
KENT...
KENT...

LET'S GO!
ROAAAR
MY POOR BABY...
SIZZLE
WHAT IS THAT THING?!
Her dragon wings spit fire!
I DON'T KNOW! BACK IN MY WORLD, SHE'S CALLED A FURIE. NOT TOO POPULAR WITH THE GUYS...
WE'VE GOT TO GET TO A STREET WHERE WE CAN FIND SOME PEOPLE...
NO WAY! WE'LL JUST BE RISKING THEIR LIVES!
GOT A BETTER PLAN?!
I'VE NEVER BEEN ANYONE'S BEFORE...
YOU'RE MINE NOW!
KENT--!
WHACK
LET GO!
AGH!!
AI!
GOTCHA! NOW YOU'RE COMING WITH ME!
.....
YOU CAN TRUST US.
LET HITA TAKE YOUR WORRIES AWAY, PRINCESS.

PRINCESS AI (TokyoPop)

trip

UGH!

KENT?!

WHAT ARE YOU DOING HERE?!

JUST LET ME... SLEEP...

Belch

SO, I LEAVE AND YOU GO OUT AND PARTY?! SOME HELP YOU ARE!

I KNEW I RECOGNIZED THAT SMELL...

-156-

!

SLOSH

NO... LIQUID ...!!

WELL, WELL...
...SO, THE LITTLE PRINCESS HAS FINALLY AWAKENED.
I REMEMBER HER...FROM AI-LAND...
I THOUGHT I'D HAVE TO BURN DOWN THE ENTIRE BUILDING BEFORE YOU SCAMPERED OUT LIKE A RAT.
ABOUT TIME I FOUND YOU!
SHE'S TESS-- ONE OF THE FURIES!
TIME TO RUN...!
!
GET THE HOSES! 
I HAVE TO DRAG THAT ROYAL BITCH BACK TO AI-LAND ALIVE-- HOW ANNOYING! IF ONLY KAZ WOULD JUST LET ME KILL HER...
I CAN'T RUN IN THIS OUTFIT...

TWILIGHT X™
STORM
JOSEPH WIGHT
01

NEOTOPIA
The ENLIGHTENED AGE
MATHENIA
PLACEA
PALLAS
1
STORY AND ART BY
ROD ESPINOSA

NEOTOPIA
The PERILOUS WINDS of ATHANON
2
STORY AND ART BY
ROD ESPINOSA

NEOTOPIA
The KINGDOMS BEYOND
3
STORY AND ART BY
ROD ESPINOSA

LEGENDS FROM
DARKWOOD
THE UNICORN HUNTERS
By CHRISTOPHER REID & JOHN KANTZ

WORLD OF HARTZ (TokyoPop)

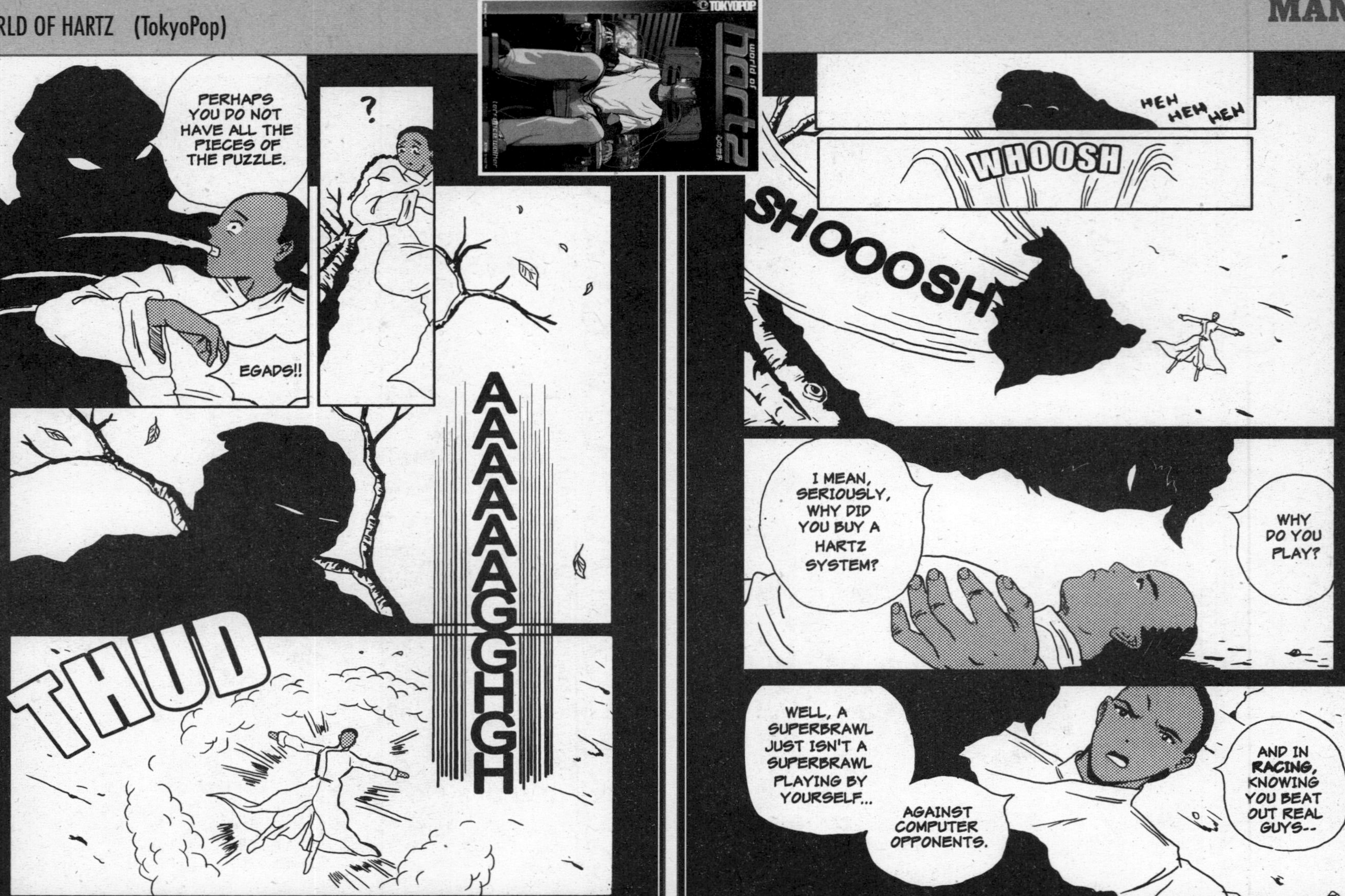
HEH HEH HEH
WHOOSH
SHOOOSH
WHY DO YOU PLAY?
I MEAN, SERIOUSLY, WHY DID YOU BUY A HARTZ SYSTEM?
AND IN RACING, KNOWING YOU BEAT OUT REAL GUYS--
WELL, A SUPERBRAWL JUST ISN'T A SUPERBRAWL PLAYING BY YOURSELF...
AGAINST COMPUTER OPPONENTS.
PERHAPS YOU DO NOT HAVE ALL THE PIECES OF THE PUZZLE.
EGADS!!
?
AAAAAAGGHGH
THUD
world of hartz
TOKYOPOP

AHHHH... BUT YOU SEE, THAT'S **YOUR** KIND OF GAME.
THE TYPE OF GAMES YOU PLAY STRESSES **COMPETITION** OVER HUMAN CONTACT.
YOU DON'T EVEN TALK TO THE PEOPLE YOU'RE FIGHTING AGAINST.
THIS TYPE OF PERSISTENT WORLD GAME IS TOTALLY DIFFERENT.
PEOPLE GATHER HERE... CREATE TEAMS AND QUEST TOGETHER.
THEY FORM FRIENDSHIPS...
AND EVEN RELATIONSHIPS.
YOU'RE SAYING HAN COULD GET SERIOUS ABOUT SOME GIRL HE'S NEVER EVEN **MET!**
IF THAT'S TRUE, THEN THIS IS WORSE THAN I **THOUGHT!**
WSSHT
IF HE GETS HER TO THAT NEXT GATE, SHE'LL SEE HIM AS SOME KIND OF **SAVIOR.**
SHE'LL PROBABLY BE STUCK ON HIM FOR GOOD.
KSHST

NATURALLY, THAT WOULDN'T HAVE BEEN A PROBLEM SINCE NEITHER ONE OF YOU COULD HAVE BEATEN THE GATE CREATURE.
UNFORTUNATELY, SHE FELL INTO A BOTTOMLESS PIT AND IS NOW **DEAD**.
THAT WASN'T SUPPOSED TO HAPPEN, BUT THEN THIS GAME **IS** AN UNFINISHED ALPHA.
WHAT CAN I DO?
CURRENTLY, THERE IS NO BOSS CHARACTER WAITING...
TO PREVENT HAN FROM GETTING THE GIRL THROUGH THE GATE.
THEY'LL JUST WALK RIGHT IN.

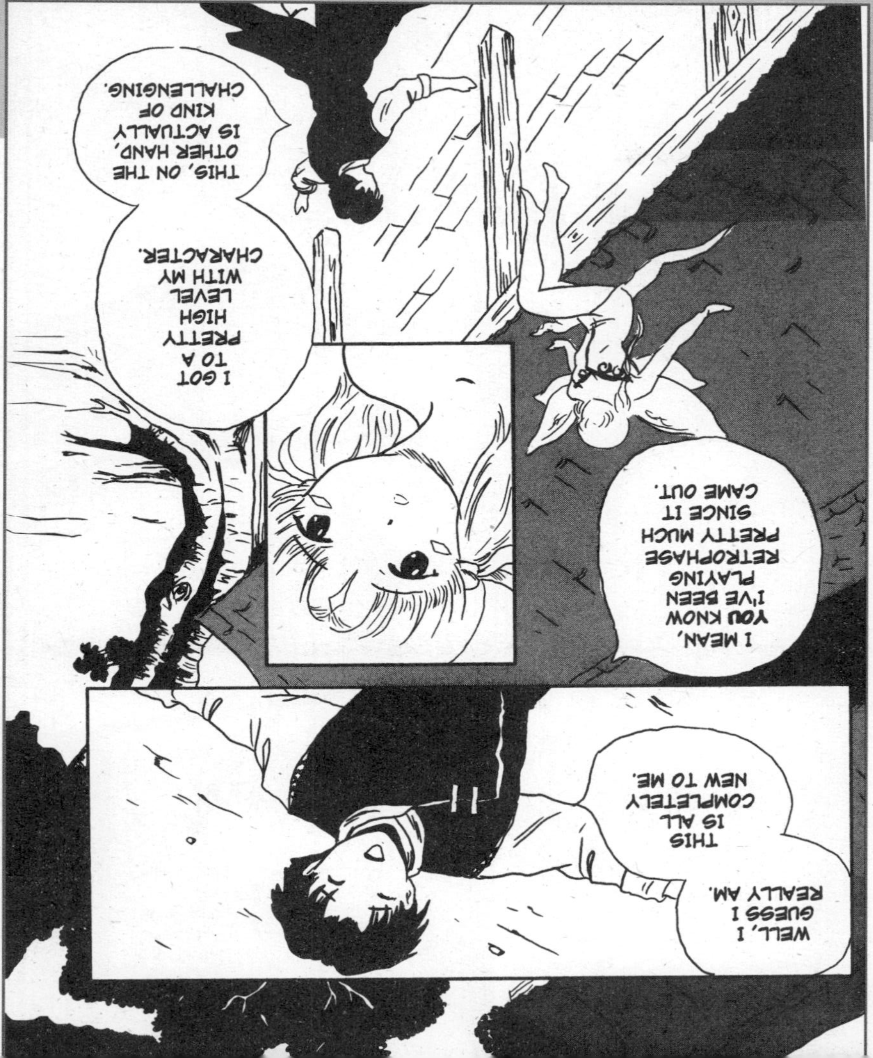

THE NEXT GATE SHOULD BE JUST UP AHEAD.

WE'RE MAKING REALLY GOOD TIME.

YOU SEEM LIKE YOU'RE HAVING FUN.

WELL, I GUESS I REALLY AM.

THIS IS ALL COMPLETELY NEW TO ME.

I MEAN, **YOU** KNOW I'VE BEEN PLAYING RETROPHASE PRETTY MUCH SINCE IT CAME OUT.

I GOT TO A PRETTY HIGH LEVEL WITH MY CHARACTER.

THIS, ON THE OTHER HAND, IS ACTUALLY KIND OF CHALLENGING.

WHOOSSHH
IN HERE, PEOPLE HAVE NO REASON TO HIDE.
TAP
DO YOU KNOW WHY THE DEVELOPERS OF THIS SYSTEM NAMED IT HARTZ?
BECAUSE IN HERE, THERE ARE NO MASKS.
WHEN YOU MEET SOMEONE ON THE STREET, THEY'RE ALWAYS WEARING A MASK.
WHETHER THEY'RE TRYING TO IMPRESS YOU, OR SELL YOU SOMETHING...
IT DOESN'T MATTER. YOU NEVER TRULY SEE THEM.

I ALWAYS SAY...
IN THIS WORLD...
...NO MASKS CAN COVER YOUR TRUE HEART.
AN OBNOXIOUS BASTARD LIKE THAT ANDRAGOTH...
CAN BE AS OBNOXIOUS AS HE WANTS TO BE.
AND WHY NOT?
FOR FEAR OF WHAT?
WHEN YOU MEET SOMEONE IN HERE...
...YOU'RE SEEING WHO THEY REALLY ARE.

WORLD OF HARTZ (TokyoPop)

BUDDHA
OSAMU TEZUKA
VOLUME
1:
Kapilavastu

BUDDHA
OSAMU TEZUKA
VOLUME
2:
The Four Encounters

RAY
AKIHITO YOSHITOMI

HARD BOILED
Angel
BLUE ANGEL 2
A CRIME NOVEL BY
HYUN SE LEE

RESERVoir CHRoNiCLE
1
TSUBASA
by
CLAMP
NEW FROM THE CREATORS OF CHOBITS!

CLAMP
CREATORS OF CHOBITS!
1
xxxHOLiC

NAMBUL
WAR STORIES
Invasion!
1
Story and Art
Hyun Se Lee

メガトーキョー
megatokyo
story & art
fred gallagher
1
story & co-creator
rodney caston

Rest of the Best

By Maureen McTigue

One of the great things about the comics medium is that it provides the ability to experiment. Whether that be with storytelling, with art style, with the size of the book, the type of paper, or going digital; whether it be the chance to move past the traditional superhero story and tell a story about a family, about growing up and old, or about technology run rampant, or all of the above in a single tale, comics offer a whole other scale of reach beyond traditional print books.

Our "Best of the Rest" section showcases this. The content is eclectic: anthologies, web comics, ashcans, small press, major publisher, self-published, Xeric-associated. A little bit of everything.

Just like comics.

The Internet, as Neil Gaiman states in his introduction, has become a broad and sturdy base for comics. Internet campaigns to save publishers have succeeded. Digital comics can be found in all shapes, sizes, styles and stories, and provide a daily, weekly or monthly respite for surfers everywhere. The two spotlighted here are Eisner-nominated... but there are so many others worth a look, beyond those graced with awards and nominations. They run the gamut from politics, to farce, to personal, to whatever-comes-to-mind. What ashcans used to be, digital comics have become and moved well-beyond.

Ashcans, the one-dollar or two-dollar photocopied comics, are still very much around. The "sampler" showcase of a larger publication, or a portfolio, or the classic mini-comic are still abundant at comic book conventions across North America. The sample spotlighted here, *Family Reunion*, exists as a self-contained story, as all good comics should, but also as an introduction to the novel *Perfect Circle*; the main character in the comic is the main character of the novel. He now lives and breathes as more than just words on the page; he is real, as real as pencil and ink and imagination will allow.

There's a cynical axiom of publishing that anthologies just won't sell, that if you give readers a collection of material by a variety of talented people, they won't go for it. Readers want, it's believed, one book driven by one person. And certainly many book buyers do routinely avoid anthologies. But, oh, what they're missing. *Sandman* became and still is a phenomena all its own—an original short-story book, telling tales of all the Endless, can do nothing but sell well.

Rest of

Table of Contents

A name writer and a group of big-name artists working on known characters is saleable and will fly off the shelves; that it happens to be good is just a bonus. We've ended the book with *Sandman* in a "bookend" fashion: Gaiman's prose lead us in, and his storytelling brings us out. The other anthology noted here is *Project: Telstar*, with a themed approach—robots in space, in this case. The book is a fantastic cross-section of potent indy talent.

Ninety Candles started out as an experiment—tell a story by creating a panel or a page to reflect each passing day. The Xeric-Award winning project shifted a bit and became a "life story" following one man's dream and life. Because in comics, you can see someone's life flash right before your eyes. Some of the other projects, like *American Elf*, *Farewell Georgia* and others are more than worth your time. They reflect life and passion and talent and the belief that what you have to say matters. They may not fall into specific categories, but these project still reflect and represent the best talent and tales the field has to offer.

DALY • BRYANT • FIDLER
ATHENA VOLTAIRE™
UPDATED MONDAY, WEDNESDAY AND FRIDAY
WWW.ATHENAVOLTAIRE.COM

... YOUR MOTHER ASKED ME TO.
YOU KNOW HOW PERSUASIVE SHE CAN BE.
AND NOW THAT THE GYPSY IS INVOLVED ...
I HAVE TO GO.
AND YOU..?
THIS VAMPIRE BITCH ATTACKED MY RANCH BEFORE SHE KNEW IF I WAS GOING TO BE INVOLVED.
I LOST THREE MEN. THREE FRIENDS.
YOU WANT THE GYPSY, I WANT HER.
WINT & RAINTREE ARE WITH ME.
ST. LEGER WANTS TO PROTECT THIS ENGLISH FAMILY ...
... AND STOP THIS WOMAN...
SO WE GO.
AND ALL THESE VAMPIRE WEIRDNESS DOESN'T BOTHER YOU?
RAFAEL, YOU AND I HAVE ENCOUNTERED MANY STRANGE THINGS.
LOOK WHAT OUR EYES HAVE SEEN... LATELY.
SANTA MARIA!
WHAT IS ALL THESE?
THESE CREATURES HAVE POWERS, ALLIES, ANIMALS —WHO KNOWS WHAT!
I INTEND TO EVEN THE PLAYING FIELD WITH SOME SURPRISES OF MY OWN.
BESIDES, PEOPLE KEEP TELLING ME I'M IN SOME KIND OF WAR ...
WELL, IT'S A WAR I'M GONNA WIN.

THE VALLEY OF THE RIVER ARGES.
"THERE, ATHENA, SEE THE BLUE MIST ON THE PEAKS..."
"...THAT'S THE MYSTICAL FLAME THAT HIDES CASTLE DRACULA FROM THE EYES OF MEN."
"AS LONG AS I CAN SEE IT WHILE I'M IN IT, DR. LEGER."
I HATE TO BREAK UP THE SIGHT-SEEING TOUR, BUT HAS ANYONE NOTICED THE WOLVES HOWLING AROUND US?
BIG WOLVES! UP ON THE CLIFF!
MANY WOLVES.
THIS IS WHY I GAVE YOU ALL FLAREGUNS.
WE'LL COUNTER HER EVERY SURPRISE.
GET READY.
FIRE!

NOW LET'S SEE IF WE CAN GET TO THE CASTLE BEFORE SHE SETS GIANT ARMADILLOS ON US.
CAN SHE... DO THAT..?

ATHENA VOLTAIRE™
DALY • BRYANT • FIDLER
UPDATED MONDAY, WEDNESDAY AND FRIDAY
WWW.ATHENAVOLTAIRE.COM

WELL, NOW I CAN SEE THE CASTLE.
MISS VOLTAIRE, A COMPANY OF MOUNTED COSSACKS AWAIT US ON THE OTHER SIDE OF THE BRIDGE.
I SAY WE CHARGE THEM!
CALDERO, YOU BROUGHT A...SWORD?!
SI. SO DID DR. LEGER. IT'S GOOD FOR LOPPING OFF THE HEADS OF VAMPIRES.

YEAH, WELL, I'VE HAD EXACTLY ONE FENCING LESSON FROM ERROL FLYNN.
I'M NOT ABOUT TO CHARGE THE BEST LIGHT CAVALRY IN THE WORLD.
I SAY WE TAKE THEM BY SURPRISE AND SHOOT 'EM!

ATHENA! ABOUT THAT SURPRISE THING...

OKAY, NOW I'M REALLY GETTING AGGRAVATED.

QUITE INGENIOUS, MISS VOLTAIRE.
BATS DON'T LIKE LIGHT...
AND YOU'VE TURNED THEIR NIGHT INTO DAY.
BUT NOW THE COSSACKS...

YES, AND NOW FOR MY NEXT SURPRISE...
I DON'T FIGHT FAIR!

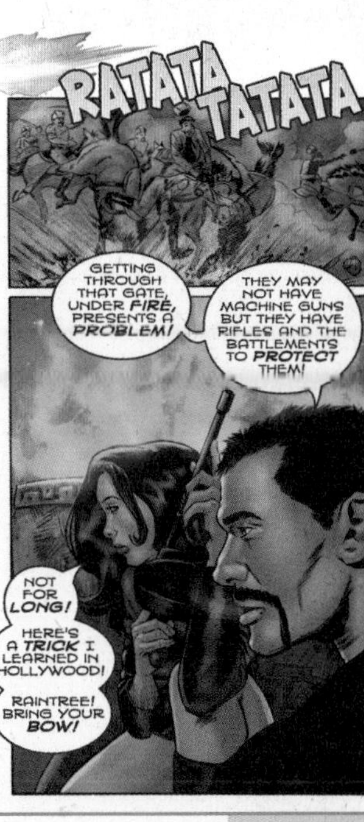
RATATA TATATA
GETTING THROUGH THAT GATE, UNDER FIRE, PRESENTS A PROBLEM!
THEY MAY NOT HAVE MACHINE GUNS BUT THEY HAVE RIFLES AND THE BATTLEMENTS TO PROTECT THEM!
NOT FOR LONG!
HERE'S A TRICK I LEARNED IN HOLLYWOOD!
RAINTREE! BRING YOUR BOW!

SSSSSLUCK!
?*!

ojingogo
by matthew forsythe

ROBOT IN THE RAIN
I CAME ACROSS HIM BY CHANCE, HUNCHED IN THE DAMP CHILL OF THE WEST LOWER 4020 LEVEL. SLEEPLESS, BEHIND IN MY WORK, LOOKING FOR CHANCE INSPIRATION, I WAS ON ONE OF MY NIGHTLY WANDERS THROUGH THE MILES OF FORGOTTEN ALLEYWAYS AND TECHNOGUTTERS BENEATH THE CITY...
AT FIRST GLANCE, HE LOOKED EXACTLY THE SAME AS ANY ONE OF THE FIFTY THOUSAND OTHER BEGGARBOTS WHICH LITTER THE CITY...
TELSTAR
I NEVER USED TO STOP FOR THESE PESTILENT, BROKEN MACHINES. I HAD MY JOB, MY WORRIES, MY DEADLINES. I HAD ENOUGH OF A LOAD!
BESIDES, I COULD NOT SAVE THEM ALL. WHAT GOOD WOULD STOPPING HAVE DONE?
I NEVER STOPPED---
...BUT THIS TIME I DID.

SOMETHING VAGUELY HUMAN IN HIS GAZE HAD ARRESTED ME. YES, JUST ANOTHER OLD ROBOT IN THE RAIN---BUT I SENSED AN EXTRA NEED, A DIFFERENT LONGING...
I STILL HALF EXPECTED THE USUAL REQUESTS FOR MONEY OR MECHANICS, BUT NONE CAME.
IT---HE?--- LOOKED ME UP AND DOWN.
THERE WAS A LONG SILENCE, A GENTLE HUM, HIS FRAME WAVERING EVER SO SLIGHTLY. THE RAIN STILL DRIPPING. A MOMENT, A SILENCE.
AFTER ANOTHER PAUSE, HE BEGAN RECITING MY LIFE BACK TO ME, RAPIDLY, IN IMPOSSIBLE DETAIL. A TORRENT OF MY SECRET FACTS AND FIGURES ALL SPILLING INTO THE WET AIR; OBVIOUS, EXPOSED, NAKED.
THERE WAS NO HINT OF COMMENTARY OR CONDEMNATION ON HIS PART. IT SEEMED SIMPLY---A DEMONSTRATION--?
YES, A DISPLAY. BUT TO WHAT END?
THEN, AT THE SAME FANTASTIC SPEED, SO QUICKLY I COULD BARELY FOLLOW, HE BEGAN TO TELL ME A STORY: AN IMPOSSIBLE TALE, ONE OF FALLEN EMPIRE, AND OF A WORLD LOST TO HUMANITY...
HE TOLD ME THE *TRUE* NAME OF EARTH, AND OF THE GLORIES OF ITS ANCIENT CIVILIZATION---WORLDWIDE SKYWAYS, BOUNTIFUL GOODS, MYRIAD ACHIEVEMENTS---
THE MERE LISTING OF IT ALL DAZZLED ME, BEWITCHED MY WRITER'S IMAGINATION...
AND THEN HE TOLD ME OF THE FALL; OF HOW OFFWORLD CONQUERORS CAME, AND OF THE WAR AND DESTRUCTION WHICH ENSUED---

HE TOLD ME OF HOW MEN, IN A DESPERATE ATTEMPT TO SURVIVE, TO PREVAIL, TOOK TO WEARING METAL SKINS, TURNING THEMSELVES INTO ROBOTS, ACQUIRING VAST POWERS BEYOND THE HUMAN...
BUT ALL THIS WAS NOT ENOUGH TO DEFEAT THE INVADERS. THE ALIENS KILLED ALL...SAVE FOR A FEW, SAVE FOR THE HIDDEN ONES.
AND THEN, INEXPLICABLY, AFTER PLUNDERING THE EMPIRE, THEY SIMPLY LEFT, SATED...
I ASKED WHEN ALL THIS HAD HAPPENED, AND HE SAID: "200 CENTURIES AGO."
I ASKED WHO HE WAS, AND HOW HE CAME TO KNOW THESE MANY THINGS...
HE REPLIED, "I WAS THEIR LEADER, AND A MAN SUCH AS YOU."
"I WAS THEIR PROTECTOR AND THEIR KING, AND IN ALL THE TIME SINCE, I HAVE WANDERED THE GLOBE, SURVIVING, SEARCHING FOR OUR LOST WEAPONS, FEARING THE INVADERS' RETURN..."
IT WAS ALL TOO FANTASTIC; I BEGAN TO LAUGH ALMOST INVOLUNTARILY, SHUDDERING IN THE COLD.
IT WAS UTTERLY *IMPOSSIBLE!*
THE WORLD WAS FULL OF ROBOTS, YES; AND MANY WERE DESTITUTE BEGGARS. BUT NONE WERE IMMORTAL, THE FALLEN KINGS OF LONG-VANISHED EMPIRES!
UNDAUNTED, HE MADE HIS APPEAL: TIME IS SHORT---WOULD I HELP HIM, SINCE HIS FRAME WAS WEAKENED, TO FIND ANY OF HIS SURVIVING LOST BRETHREN, HIS SUBJECTS... TO ASSEMBLE, TO ORGANIZE... TO PREPARE?
I REMEMBER IT ALL SO WELL, THAT MOMENT, NOW AND FOREVER...THE CONSTANT DAMP CHILL, THE DISTANT HUSH OF THE HOVERWAYS, THE SMELL OF ANCIENT METAL...
...BUT GOD HELP ME, I LAUGHED AGAIN, AND SAID: "*PREPARE FOR WHAT?*"

"THEY RETURN," HE SAID. "I AM DYING, AND I MUST FIND A REPLACEMENT---TO CONTINUE THE FIGHT!" AND THEN HE TOLD ME OF A CERTAIN EVENT WHICH WOULD OCCUR THAT VERY NIGHT, THE FIRST SMALL STEP OF THE ALIENS' RETURN...
AND HE SHOWED ME YET MORE, INSIDE THE WALLS OF MY MIND, OF ALL THE HORRORS WHICH WOULD COME TO PASS. HE SAW IT ALL WITH HIS POWERS, YET WITHOUT HELP COULD NOT STOP IT...
I GASPED, BUT HE SEEMED TO MISTAKE THIS FOR THE COMING OF MORE LAUGHTER, AND SO GREW ANGRY. BEFORE I COULD SAY MORE, HIS GAZE ALTERED---
---AND WITH NOTHING FURTHER, HE BEGAN MOVING AWAY.
I GRASPED AT HIM, BUT SLIPPED--- SLIPPED ON THE WRETCHED PAVEMENT!
AND THEN SILENTLY, FINALLY, HE WAS LOST IN THE GLOOM...
I TRUDGED HOME, TO MY FLAT, TO MY DINNER, HOPING IT WOULD NOT HAPPEN AS HE SAID.
BUT THAT FIRST NIGHT, ALL HIS PREDICTIONS, AND MORE, CAME TRUE.
THE NEXT NIGHT---NOTHING! IT ALL STOPPED.
I HAD NO WAY TO DETERMINE IF IT WAS ALL A BIZARRE MISTAKE, OR A HOAX--- THE CHANCE MAD RAVINGS OF A BROKEN, SOAKED PROCESSOR. PERHAPS IT WAS... YET...HE HAD KNOWN MY *LIFE!*
HOW?
I HAD TO FIND HIM AGAIN! I RAN BACK TO HIS CRACKED DOORWAY, BUT THERE WAS ONLY RAIN AND SILENCE...
AND NOW...
...AND NOW I WANDER THE ENDLESS LEVELS OF THE CITY, SEARCHING FOR A LOST KING WHO MAY STILL HOLD THE KEYS TO OUR SALVATION---
I RETURN OVER AND OVER AGAIN TO THE SAME RUINED PLACES, YET ALWAYS FIND... NOTHING...
BUT I MUST FIND HIM, JUST ONE ROBOT!
ONE ROBOT, STANDING FORGOTTEN IN A DOORWAY...
ONE BROKEN ROBOT IN THE RAIN, TELLING AN IMPOSSIBLE TALE...

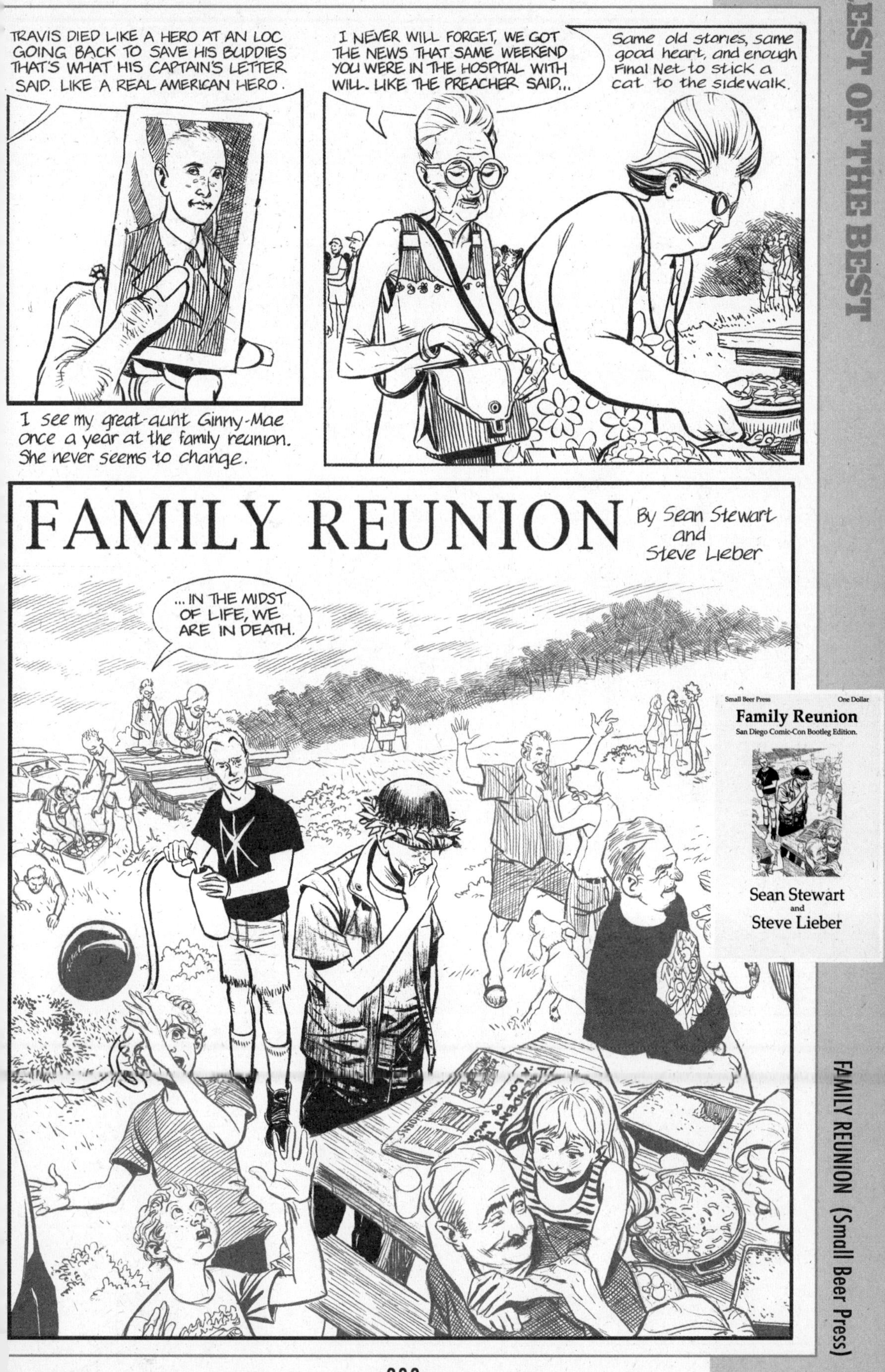

TRAVIS DIED LIKE A HERO AT AN LOC GOING BACK TO SAVE HIS BUDDIES THAT'S WHAT HIS CAPTAIN'S LETTER SAID. LIKE A REAL AMERICAN HERO.

I see my great-aunt Ginny-Mae once a year at the family reunion. She never seems to change.

I NEVER WILL FORGET, WE GOT THE NEWS THAT SAME WEEKEND YOU WERE IN THE HOSPITAL WITH WILL. LIKE THE PREACHER SAID...
Same old stories, same good heart, and enough Final Net to stick a cat to the sidewalk.

FAMILY REUNION

By Sean Stewart and Steve Lieber

...IN THE MIDST OF LIFE, WE ARE IN DEATH.

Small Beer Press One Dollar

Family Reunion

San Diego Comic-Con Bootleg Edition.

Sean Stewart and Steve Lieber

Most people think of ghosts as... vapor. Dreams.
Houston Chronicle
PRESIDENT TO TROOPS:
A LOT OF WORK LEFT TO DO
LONGHORNS

They're not. They're more real than you are.

WILL, WOULD YOU HELP ME BRING OUT THE BIG ICEBOX?

"WILL?"
ICEBOX?

GOOD PLAN, MOM. WE DEFINITELY NEED MORE FOOD OUT HERE.
I NEED ME A TIME-OUT FROM GINNY-MAE. I LOVE HER TO DEATH, BUT SHE DOES LIKE TO TO TALK

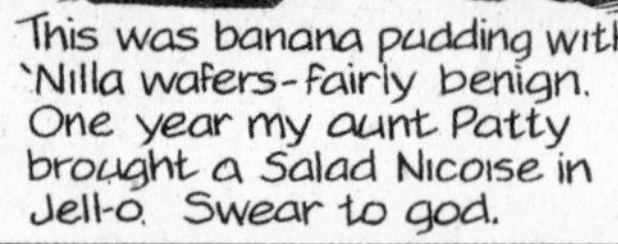
This was banana pudding with 'Nilla wafers-fairly benign. One year my aunt Patty brought a Salad Nicoise in Jell-o. Swear to god.

THAT BOY OF HERS HAS BEEN WITH THE LORD THIRTY-TWO YEARS. I JUST WISH...

"...I JUST WISH SHE COULD LET HIM GO..."

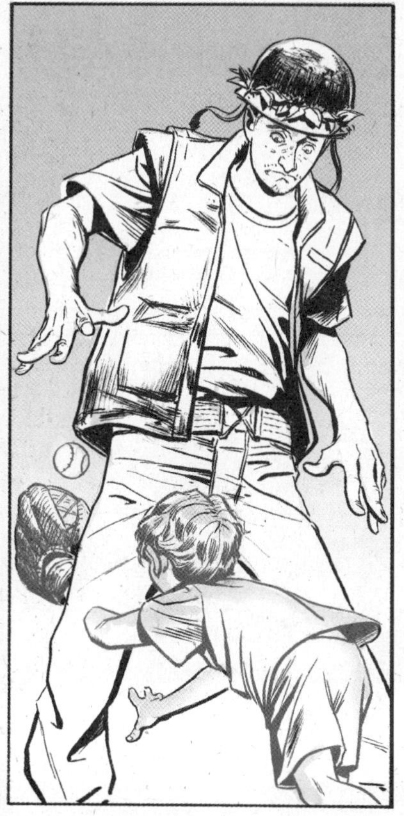

THAT'S GOTTA SUCK...
HEY THERE, PARDNER

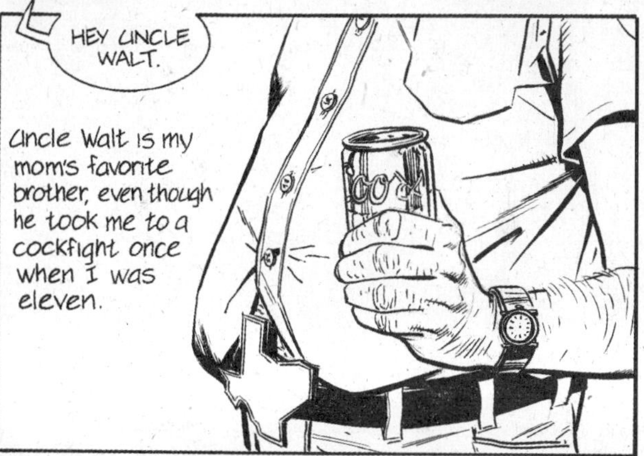
HEY UNCLE WALT.
Uncle Walt is my mom's favorite brother, even though he took me to a cockfight once when I was eleven.

WHAT YOU PUT UP ON THE SCOREBOARD SINCE THE LAST REUNION?
FIRED: TWO LAID: ZERO

DAMN, SON. WELL...
...IT AIN'T OVER 'TIL IT'S OVER.
YEAH
And sometimes not even then.

DO I REMEMBER THERE WAS A COUSIN ENLISTED SAME TIME AS YOU?
YESSIR. GINNIE MAE'S BOY. HE DIDN'T ENLIST, THOUGH. HIS DRAFT NUMBER JUST CAME UP.

"SHOULD HAVE GOT A DEFERMENT. HE HAD HIM A BASEBALL SCHOLARSHIP AT AUSTIN."
HOOK 'EM HORNS
"BUT HE BUSTED UP WITH HIS GIRLFRIEND THE NIGHT BEFORE HIS EXAMS."

WHO THE HELL IS THIS GUY?
WHAT ARE YOU DOING? SPYING ON ME?
HEY MAN, LIKE..."HOOK 'EM HORNS!"

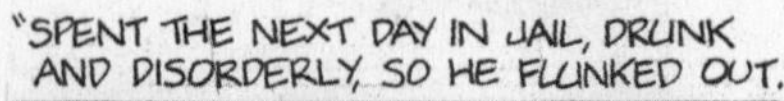
"SPENT THE NEXT DAY IN JAIL, DRUNK AND DISORDERLY, SO HE FLUNKED OUT."

"GIRLFRIEND TOOK HIM BACK BUT BY THAT TIME, THE SERVICE GOT HIM."

"HE WAS ONE OF THOSE DISCONTENTED FELLAS."
"WHEREVER HE WAS, THAT'S THE ONE SPOT HE DIDN'T WANT TO BE AT."

SOMETHING'S WAITING UP THERE.
IT'S NOT WHAT YOU CAN SEE COMING THAT GETS YOU...

"...THE SERIOUS SHIT IS ALREADY THERE, SNEAKING UP ON YOU FROM BEHIND."
"COYOTE?" WHAT THE HELL KIND OF NAME IS "COYOTE?"
women is bitches

ABOUT THE TIME YOU WERE FIXING TO COME INTO THE WORLD, THE VC PUT A BIG PUSH ON AN LOC.

"THEY OVER-RAN THE CAMP WHERE TRAVIS WAS. HE KILLED ABOUT A DOZEN OF THEM WITH HAND-GRENADES, THROWING **REAL** HIGH HEAT."

"FINALLY GOT PICKED OFF GOING BACK TO RESCUE A BUDDY."

"GINNIE MAE FRAMED THE LETTER THAT CAPTAIN OF HIS WROTE ABOUT IT AND HUNG IT ON HER WALL."

WHY'D YOU COME TO ASK, ANYWAY? DID YOU-
NAH, JUST CURIOUS.
As far as seeing dead people goes, the family and me are pretty much Don't ask, Don't tell.
LOOKING FOR SOMETHING?
OH, UH- I WAS JUST LOOKING FOR MEGAN. I WANTED TO GET ME SOME SUGAR FROM THAT DAUGHTER OF YOURS.
SHE'S WITH HER MOM. IT'S NOT ONE OF MY WEEKENDS.

I SURE WAS SORRY ABOUT YOU AND JOSIE. I DIDN'T SEE THAT COMING.
ME NEITHER.

WHAT THE HELL ARE YOU LOOKING AT?
WHAT DO YOU WANT, ANYWAY?

Houston Chronic
PRESIDENT TO TROOP
A LOT OF WORK LEFT T
Longhorns

I LOOK LIKE I WORK FOR THE U.N. OR SOMETHING? I CAN'T DO ANYTHING ABOUT THAT.

OH.
Longhorns

Longhorn
bound for
College World
Series

HOOK 'EM HORNS.

37.

"THANKS FOR THE SKETCH, KEV - OH, AND THE BOOK IS GREAT! INSPIRATIONAL!"

"THINK YOU'LL GET AN EISNER? YOU MUST BE REALLY HAPPY!"

38.

"OF COURSE YOU SHOULD VOTE FOR YOURSELF! YOU THINK CHRIS WARE ISN'T MARKING HIS BOX?"

"C'MON, KEVIN... BE SELFISH FOR A CHANGE."

39.

"NO, MOM... THE AWARD-WINNING CARTOONIST IS TELLING HIS SON A BEDTIME STORY."

"NO, HE DOESN'T KNOW WHAT HIS NEXT PROJECT IS. HE'S HAD SOME OFFERS... WE'LL LET YOU KNOW."

40.

"WELL, THEY SAY THE THIRD DRAFT'S THE CHARM. IT'S YOUR FIRST SCREENPLAY - NO BIGGIE."

"RELAX NOW... WORK ON YOUR NEW BOOK. YOU DO HAVE ANOTHER BOOK COMING OUT, RIGHT?"

41.

"I DON'T KNOW - JUST DON'T DRAW ONE ABOUT ME!"

"I KNOW YOUR PUBLISHER WANTS ANOTHER BOOK... BUT I CAN'T HELP YOU COME UP WITH IDEAS."

"WHADDYA MEAN 'OUT OF PRODUCTION CAPITAL?' FIND SOME! NO... DON'T TELL ME THE MOVIE'S KILLED... OF COURSE HE'S WORKING ON ANOTHER BOOK- THAT'S NOT THE POINT! WE HAD A DEAL."

"YOU ARE WORKING ON ANOTHER BOOK, RIGHT?"

43.

"MAYBE TAKING A BREAK TO PLAY CATCH IS A GOOD IDEA, KEVIN."

"YOU'VE BEEN STARING AT THAT BLANK PAGE ALL DAY..."

44.

"YOU KNOW I THINK YOUR STUFF IS BOSS, KEV... BUT WE'VE ALLOCATED OUR PUBLISHING CAPITAL TO DEAN AND JAMES THIS YEAR... AND AUTOBIO ISN'T THE DRAW IT USED TO BE..."

"HAVE YOU SPOKEN TO THE LOWRIDER GUYS?"

• WE WERE NOT MADE FOR THIS WORLD •

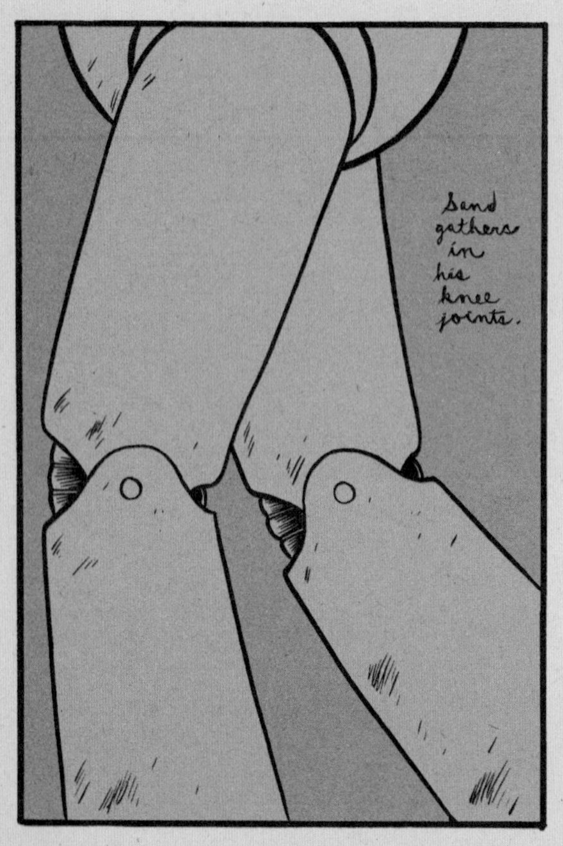
Sand gathers in his knee joints.

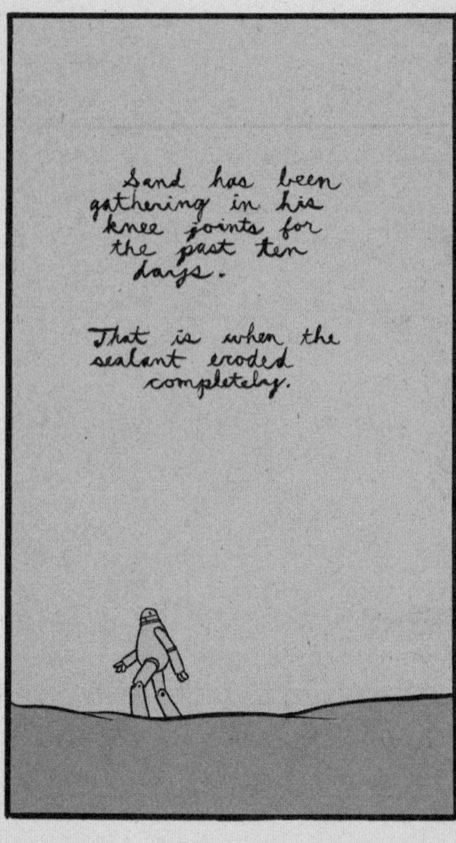
Sand has been gathering in his knee joints for the past ten days.
That is when the sealant eroded completely.

Sand gathers in his knee joints at sixteen to thirty-two granules per minute, depending on wind speed.
Eight to ten are forced out by the still functioning internal defenses...

... but clearly this leaves accumulation.

With effort he modifies his walking method, taking more abbreviated steps, allowing less exposure of the vulnerable area.

Now there is slightly less accumulation...
... but still ground is lost.

He is sharply aware he may not reach his destination.

If such a destination even exists.

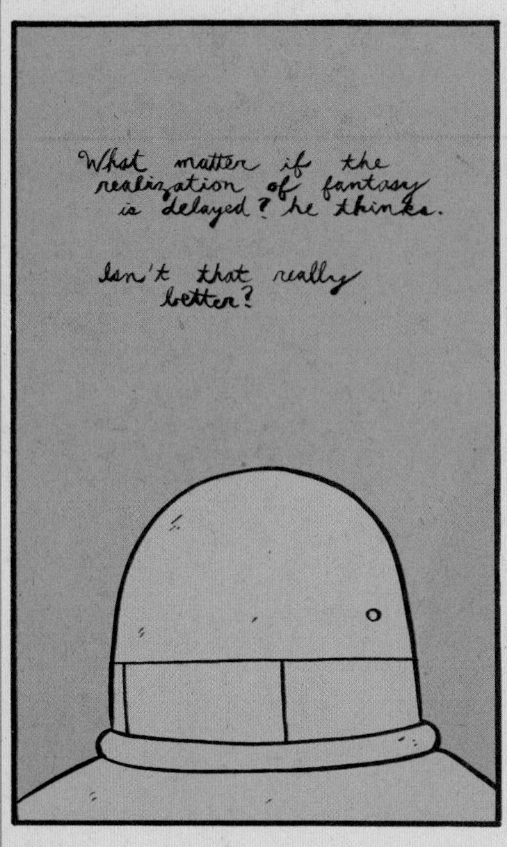
What matter if the realization of fantasy is delayed? he thinks.
Isn't that really better?

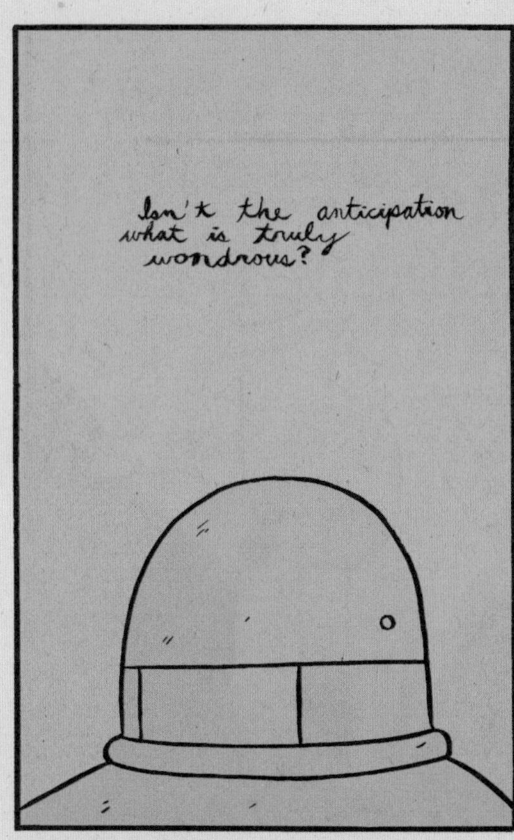
Isn't the anticipation what is truly wondrous?

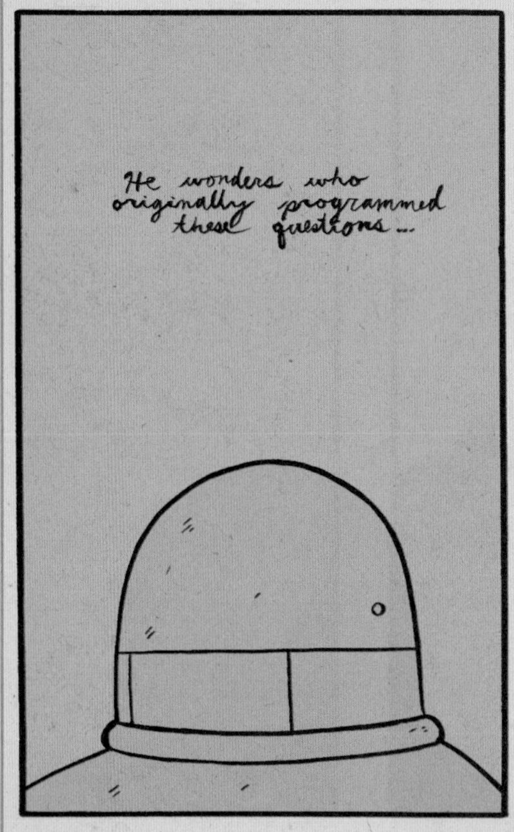
He wonders who originally programmed these questions...

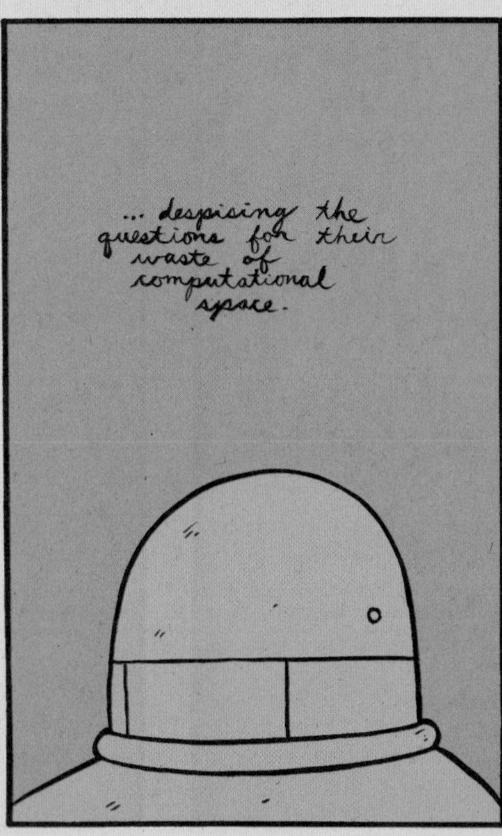
...despising the questions for their waste of computational space.

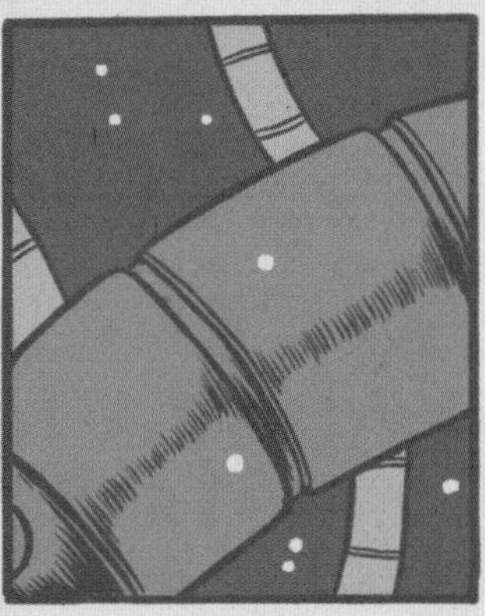

Another minute passes
and another seventeen
granules come in.
Nine are pushed out.
He focuses on the
horizon and tries
to think it is beautiful.

Somewhere along this line of the horizon, he theorizes is a place where they still exist.

The things that built the Assembly and the City.

Series and series ago, somewhere
something had to have built
them, or so he reasoned.

And
perhaps
these things
would explain
why
they built
them.
And perhaps
it would explain
everything.

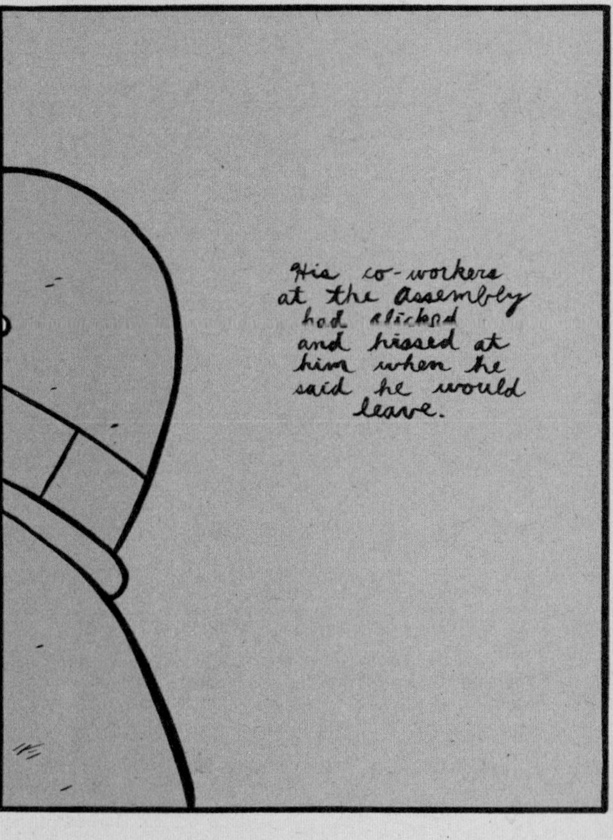
His co-workers
at the Assembly
had clicked
and hissed at
him when he
said he would
leave.

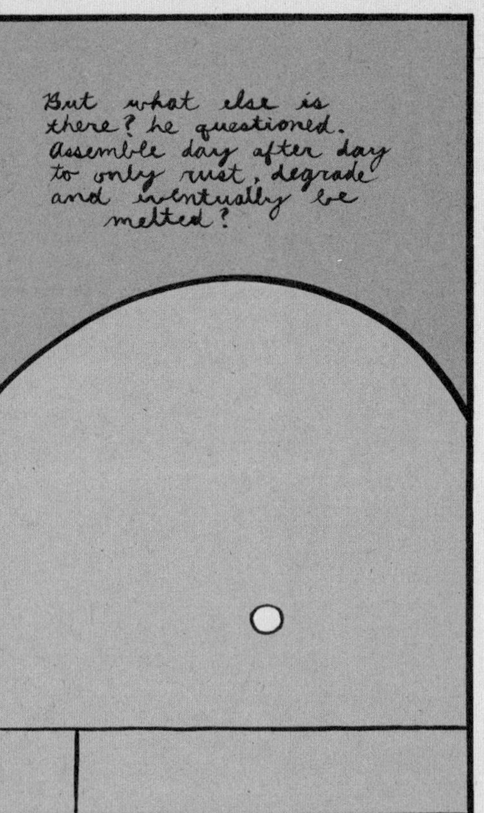
But what else is
there? he questioned.
Assemble day after day
to only rust, degrade
and eventually be
melted?

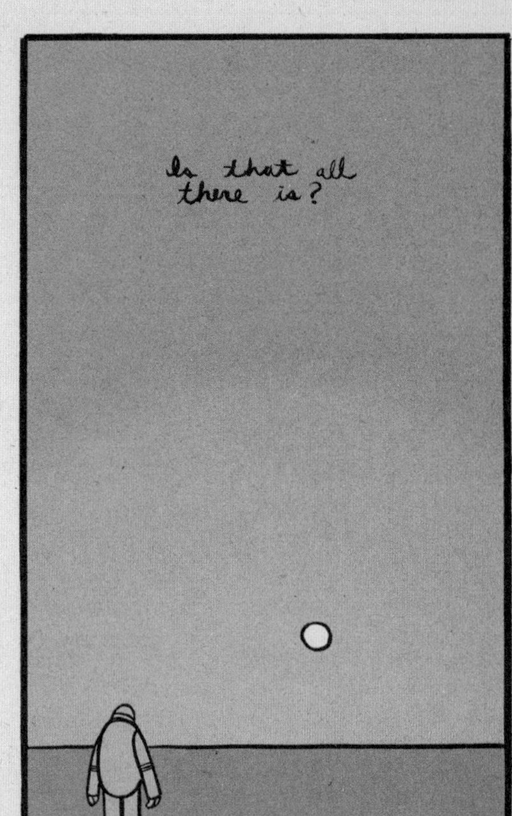
Is that all
there is?

He found it impossible to accept and they found him impossible to accept.

And so he left.

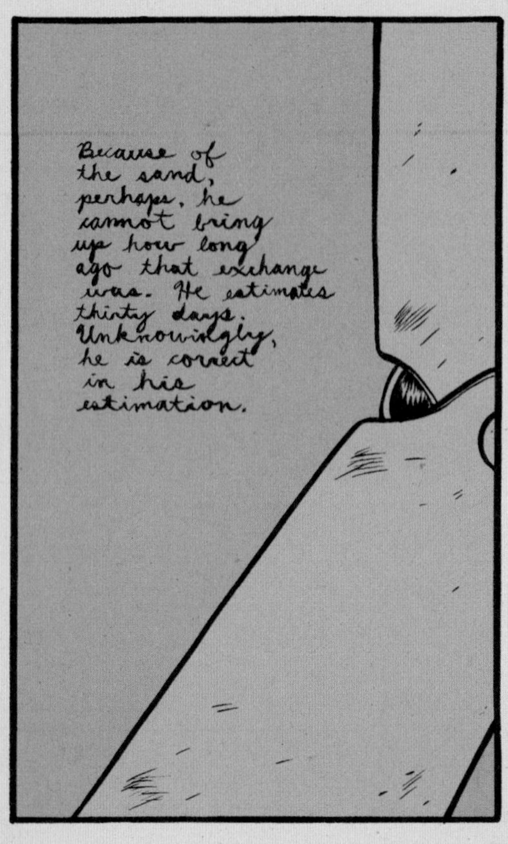
Because of the sand, perhaps, he cannot bring up how long ago that exchange was. He estimates thirty days. Unknowingly, he is correct in his estimation.

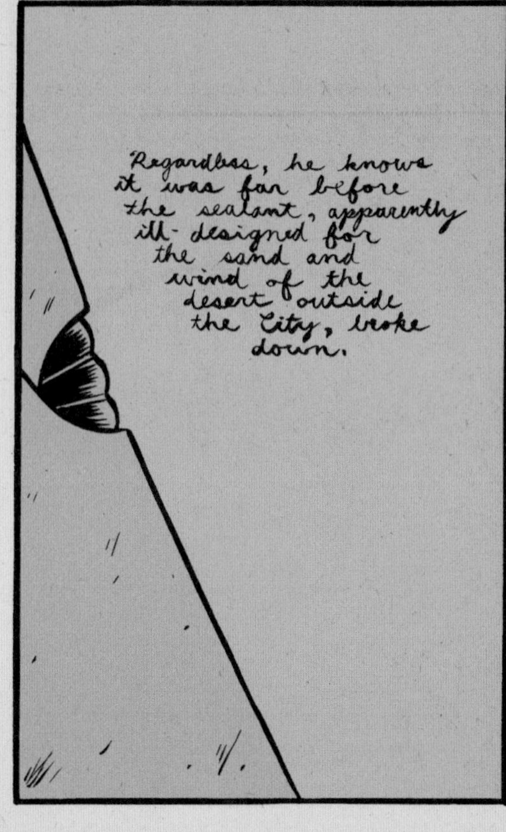
Regardless, he knows it was far before the sealant, apparently ill-designed for the sand and wind of the desert outside the City, broke down.

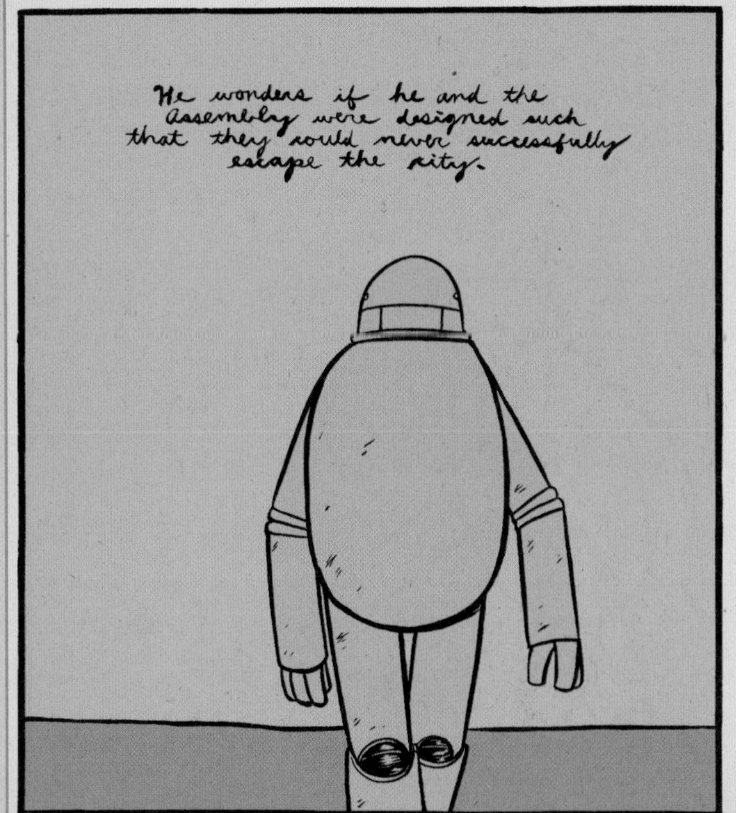
He wonders if he and the Assembly were designed such that they could never successfully escape the city.

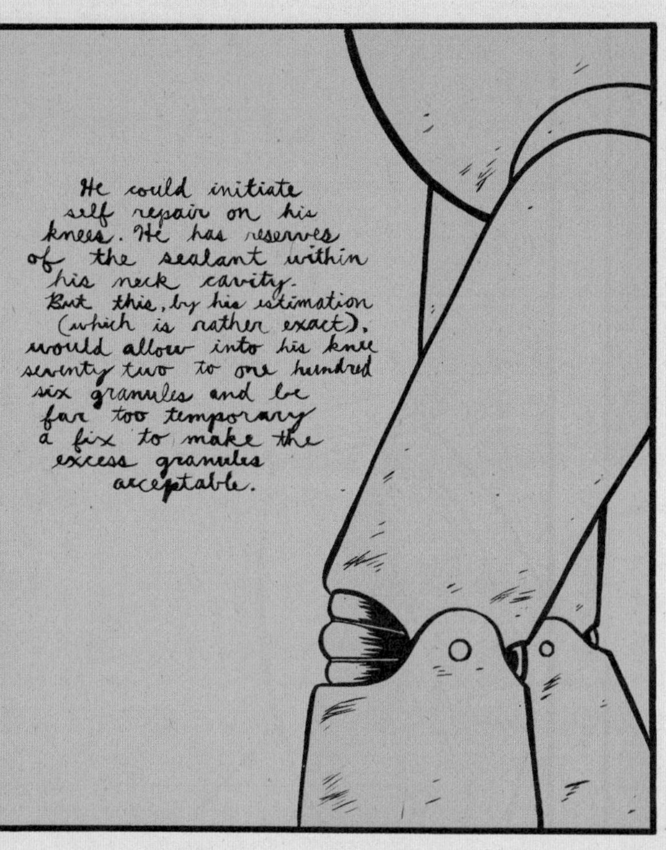
He could initiate self repair on his knees. He has reserves of the sealant within his neck cavity. But this, by his estimation (which is rather exact), would allow into his knee seventy two to one hundred six granules and be far too temporary a fix to make the excess granules acceptable.

He estimates he will not be able to walk within a week.

He continues his abbreviated steps.

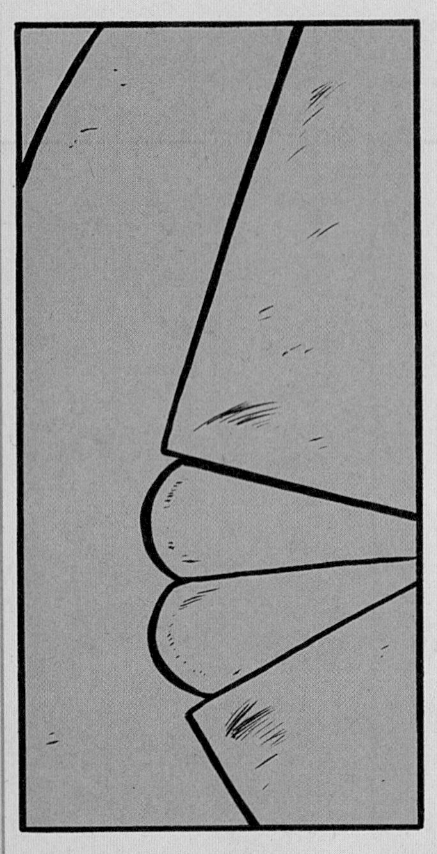

He begins a diagnostic on his elbows, wondering how long his arms can carry him after his legs have failed to do so.

another minute passes
and another twenty-two granules come in.

Eight are pushed out.

He focuses on the horizon and tries to think it is beautiful.

They've been parting visitors from their money for so long here in Venice that they can't help but be good at it. Normally, they give value for money. That last encounter left a sour taste in my mouth. They didn't cheat the tourists when I came here as a boy.
And that starts me remembering once again.

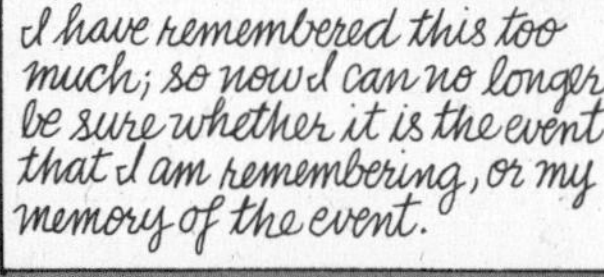
I have remembered this too much; so now I can no longer be sure whether it is the event that I am remembering, or my memory of the event.

A hot, still day. Lizards, on the side of a brick wall, watch me warily.

You could catch them, if you were fast enough. But if you grabbed them by the tail it would break off, wriggling, in your hand, while the lizard ran away.
I had been staying with my aunt and uncle, with my cousins. My Italian was not good, but I could make myself understood, and we all spoke some English.

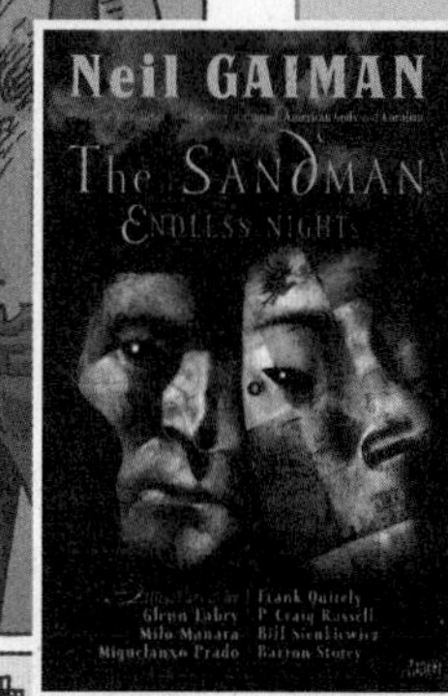
Neil GAIMAN
The SANDMAN
ENDLESS NIGHTS
Frank Quitely
Glenn Fabry
P. Craig Russell
Milo Manara
Bill Sienkiewicz
Miguelanxo Prado
Barron Storey

We loaded the picnic food and the bottles of fruit-juice and the wine into my Uncle's vaporetto, the water-taxi he drove, and we travelled out into the lagoon until we reached the island.

There are many islands in the Venice Lagoon. Over the years they have all been inhabited, my Uncle told me, as I proudly steered the boat. But times change. He pointed out the islands that hold factories, barracks, munitions, convents, as we passed.

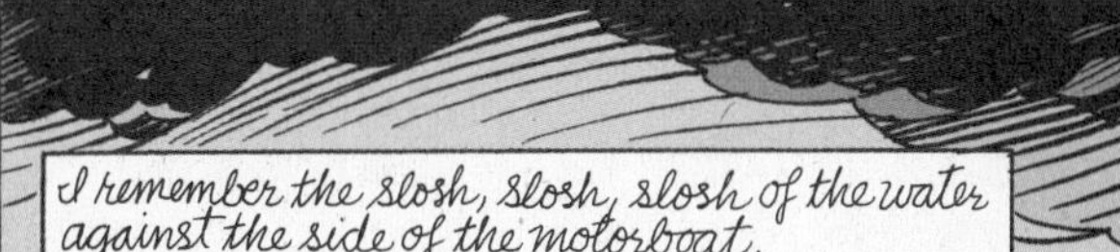
I remember the slosh, slosh, slosh of the water against the side of the motorboat.

WHEN I WAS A YOUNG MAN, IN THE ARMY, WE WERE STATIONED ON THIS ISLAND. ON THE NORTH SIDE IS AN OLD MONASTERY.
NOW IS ALL RUINS. BUT IS A GOOD PLACE FOR A PICNIC.
YOU KEEP AWAY FROM THE RUINS. THEY WILL BE DANGEROUS.
YES, UNCLE.

We all ate bread and fish and fruit and chocolate. We drank apricot juice, the adults drank wine. Then my Aunt and Uncle sat beneath an old fig tree and read a book or dozed, and sent us to play, with one final warning to keep well away from any ruins.

We played hide-and-seek across the southern half of the island, clambering over ruined walls.

I grew bored with the game, or perhaps my cousins had hidden themselves too well.

I kept walking...

HELLO, SERGEI.
HAVE YOU SEEN ANY OTHER KIDS AROUND HERE, LIKE ME? WE WERE PLAYING.
I HAVEN'T SEEN ANYBODY HERE IN A LONG TIME.
It didn't seem strange to me that she knew my name, or that she talked my language.
WHAT ARE YOU DOING?
WATCHING THAT GATE. I'M WAITING FOR THE DAY THAT IT OPENS.
WELL, WHY DON'T YOU JUST GO AROUND IT?
THAT WOULDN'T BE FAIR. AND WHAT MAKES YOU THINK THAT I'D REACH THE SAME PLACE IF I WENT AROUND IT?
IT WON'T OPEN.
IT'S LOCKED.
OR IT'S RUSTED SHUT.

I CAN WAIT.
MMM FFF
SERGEI!
WHERE WERE YOU?
WHY DIDN'T YOU COME WHEN WE CALLED?
WE LOOKED FOR HOURS! PAPA IS FURIOUS!
Somehow, it was nearly dark. I had been missing for hours. I said I had fallen asleep, and perhaps it was true. I was in disgrace, and remained so for the remainder of my stay.
In time, I came to believe I had imagined the whole thing. And now, on two weeks' leave from my unit, I am in Venice once again.

AT NINE IN THE MORNING, THE COUNT AROSE AND DECLARED FOR THAT EVENING A MASKED BALL OF UNPARALLELED SPLENDOR AND MAGNIFICENCE.
CASKS OF SHERRY WERE BROUGHT UP FROM THE CELLARS, ALONG WITH BOTTLES OF THE FINEST WINES.
ANIMALS WERE SLAUGHTERED AND SPITTED.
COSTUMES WERE EXAMINED, MASKS WERE PURCHASED AND REPAIRED. THE WORD WAS SENT TO VENICE, AND THE SURROUNDING ISLANDS.

AT 3:02 PM A FLOCK OF SNOW-WHITE DOVES ROSE INTO THE AIR AND FLEW ACROSS THE ISLAND.

AT DUSK, A FLOTILLA OF BOATS, EACH WITH A LANTERN IN THE PROW, PULLED UP IN THE BAY...

...DISCHARGING SEVERAL DOZEN WOMEN, MASKED AND EXQUISITELY DRESSED.

NOBLEWOMEN!
SOME WHISPERED.
COURTESANS!
SAID OTHERS.
NUNS, FROM THE CONVENT OF SAN MICHELE DI MURANO, HERE IN DEFIANCE OF THEIR VOWS...
WHISPERED THOSE WHO HAD SCULLED THE OARS.

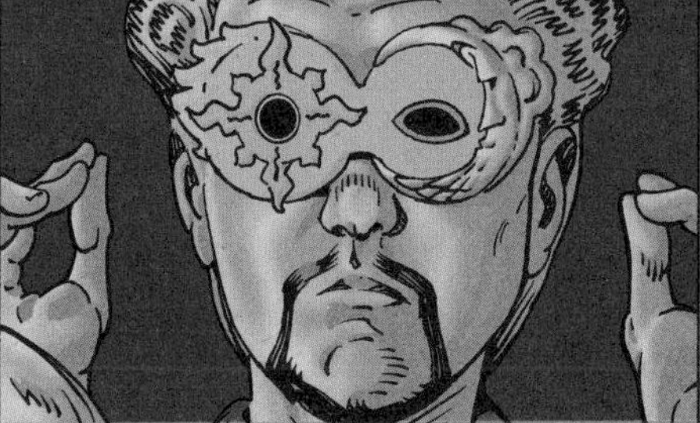

EACH REVELLER, MORE RESPLENDENT THAN THE LAST, WAS A SYMPHONY IN BLUE, A CONFECTION IN SCARLET, A STUDY IN OLIVE OR VERMILION OR WHITE, FOR THE COUNT HAD DECREED THAT THE COLOR BLACK WAS FORBIDDEN ON HIS ISLAND.
IT CARRIED OVERTONES WITH WHICH HE WAS NOT ENTIRELY COMFORTABLE.
WHAT ARE YOU THINKING, MY LORD ABBOT?
I AM THINKING THAT YOUR WINE IS GOOD, SIRE.
AND THE DAY? WHAT DID YOU THINK OF THE DAY?
THE DAY, AS ALWAYS, IS PERFECT.
MY FRIENDS!
MY LOVED ONES!
MY ENEMIES.
WE LIVE IN A PERFECT TIME, HERE IN OUR DAY. WE LOVE, WE FIGHT, WE GAMBLE, WE DRINK, WE DO ALL WE DO IN OUR PERFECT DAY, UNTOUCHED BY TIME, UNTAKEN BY DEATH.
HERE, IN OUR DAY, JUDGMENT DAY WILL COME AND GO, AND THE SUN WILL FLARE INTO NOTHINGNESS, A COLD CINDER, AND STILL WE SHALL HAVE FINE WEATHER, AND ALL THE WEALTH AND RESOURCES OF THE REPUBLIC OF VENICE TO DRAW UPON.
TOMORROW, THE INQUISITION WILL ARRIVE, TO INVESTIGATE MY ALCHEMICAL RESEARCHES. TOMORROW THE COUNCIL OF TEN WILL CALL FOR ME TO BE IMPRISONED BENEATH THE LEADS. BUT THAT TOMORROW WILL NEVER COME...
A TOAST!
TO OUR ISLAND!
...AND TO OUR PERFECT DAY!

DOES THIS VAPORETTO GO OUT TO THE ISLANDS?
IT GOES ANYWHERE, AS LONG AS YOU PAY. YOU WANT A TOUR OF THE ISLANDS?
MY BROTHER CAN MAKE YOU GOOD DEAL FOR GLASS ON MURANO.
I told him which island I wanted him to take me to, then described where it was to the best of my recollection.

MM. IF YOU WISH. BUT IT IS DESERTED. THERE ARE NO STORES, NO RESTAURANTS, NOTHING FOR A VISITOR TO SEE. AND IN THIS WEATHER...
I KNOW.
I'LL PAY.

So he took my money, and the vaporetto, the water taxi, sped through the canals of Venice on its way to the lagoon.

From the canals, you can see the damage the rising water levels is doing to the city.
History, I thought, accretes in Venice like silt in a canal...

...and it laps against the bricks and rocks and the deep wooden piles.

And as we ride, I find myself wondering: If my life would have been different—if, say, I had not gone to the island as a boy.

Would I have stayed with Patricia?

Would I have joined the army, applied for the unit I applied for?

Perhaps I would still be with Patricia, if, at each kiss, at every touch, I had not compared her to the woman on the island.

Her eyes were not so dark and sparkling.

Her smile was never so haunting.

I channel that longing for something I cannot reach into my job. I do it efficiently.
Someone has to.

I tell the vaporetto driver to wait for me.

HELLO. YOU CAME BACK, I THOUGHT YOU WOULD.
Everything moved slowly when I saw her. The rain seemed to fall gently, like snowflakes.
YOU KNOW, I ALMOST THOUGHT I HAD IMAGINED YOU.

NO. I'M REAL.
DO YOU COME OUT HERE EVERY DAY? OR DO YOU LIVE HERE ON THE ISLAND?

I GET AROUND. YOU KNOW, YOU'RE THE FIRST PERSON EVER TO COME BACK.
DO YOU REMEMBER WHAT YOU DID THE LAST TIME YOU WERE HERE?

I TRIED TO OPEN THE GATE.

WOULD YOU LIKE TO TRY AGAIN?

YOU KNOW, THERE'S PROBABLY SOME LAW PROTECTING HISTORICAL REMAINS.

I pulled. It was set fast into the brick. I was angry with myself, I thought, I should have brought a sledge-hammer, or a crowbar, or a wrecking ball.
Then I thought to kick it.

And kicking that damned gate seemed suddenly to be the most satisfying thing I could do.

I was kicking at my life.
At my family.
At my unit.
At death, at time, at every lie I had ever been told.

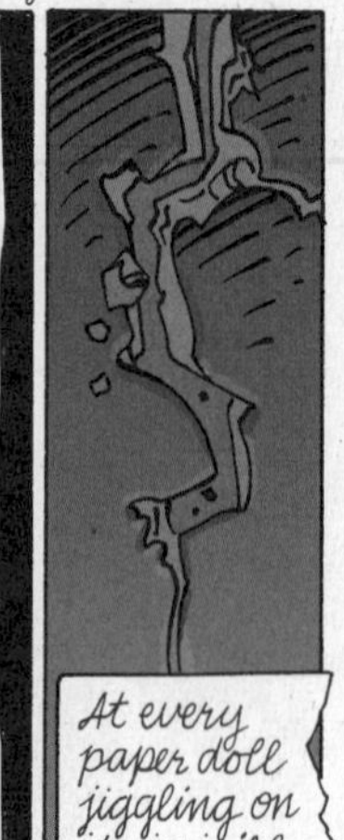
At every paper doll jiggling on its invisible string...

YOU DID IT!
WHERE ARE WE?
MAY THE 23rd, 1751.
THAT'S A WHEN, NOT A WHERE.

HERE, IT'S A WHERE.
CAN YOU WAIT HERE?
I HAVE BUSINESS INSIDE.

I WANT TO COME WITH YOU.
OKAY. I GUESS.

SANDMAN (Vertigo/DC Comics)

YOU WANT TO BLEND IN, DON'T YOU? COME ON, LET'S SPOIL THE PARTY.

YOU LOOK MOST LOVELY, YOUNG LADY.
WILL YOU WALK WITH ME?

ONLY FOR A LITTLE WHILE, GIUSEPPE. YOU DIED OF SYPHILIS IN 1768, IN AN ATTIC IN TRIESTE.

HE DROWNED IN A STORM.

SHE DIED IN CHILD-BIRTH.

AS AN OLD MAN, HE CHOKED ON A BONE IN A BOWL OF FISH SOUP.

SANDMAN (Vertigo/DC Comics)

A

AGE OF BRONZE

All contents copyright © 2004 by Eric Shanower. All Rights Reserved. AGE OF BRONZE™, Linear B, and all characters and their distinctive likenesses are trademarks of Eric Shanower. Published by Image Comics. www.imagecomics.com/

AMERICAN ELF: THE COLLECTED SKETCHBOOK DIARIES OF JAMES KOCHALKA

© 2004 By James Kochalka. Published by Top Shelf Productions, Brett Warnock and Chris Staros. All Rights Reserved. www.topshelfcomix.com/

ARTESIA AFIRE

Artesia is © and TM 1999 Mark. S. Smylie. Artesia Afire is © 2004 Mark S. Smylie. The Book of Dooms is © and TM 2003 Mark S. Smylie. The ASP logo is TM 2003 Archaia Studios Press. All Rights Reserved. Published by Archaia Studios Press. www.artesiaonline.com/

ASTONISHING X-MEN

by Joss Whedon, John Cassaday and Laura Martin © 2004 Marvel Characters, Inc. Published by Marvel Comics, a division of Marvel Entertainment Group, Inc. marvel.com/

ATHENA VOLTAIRE

Athena Voltaire is a trademark of Steve Bryant and Paul Daly. © 2005 Steve Bryant & Paul Daly. Found online at www.athenavoltaire.com/

B

BATMAN

© 2003 DC Comics. All Rights Reserved. Published by DC Comics dccomics.com/

BLACKSAD

Written by Juan Diaz, illustrated by Guarnido. Copyright © 2003 Dargaud, Juan Diaz Canales and Juanjo Guarnido. All Rights Reserved. Published by ibooks, inc. www.komikwerks.com/

BLAB 14

All stories, artwork, and illustration © copyright 2003 by the respective artists unless otherwise indicated. Published by Fantagraphics Books. fantagraphics.com/

BLANKETS

© 2004, 2003 Craig Thompson. Published by Top Shelf Productions, Brett Warnock and Chris Staros. All rights reserved.

BOMBABY: THE SCREEN GODDESS

by Antony Mazzotta. Bombaby is ™ and © 2003 Antony Mazzotta. All Rights Reserved. Published by SLG Publishing. www.slavelabor.com/

BUDDHA BY OSAMU TEZUKA

© 2004 Tezuka Productions. Published by Vertical, Inc. www.vertical-inc.com/

C

CLYDE FANS

by Seth © 2004 by G. (Seth) Gallant. All Rights Reserved. Published by Drawn & Quarterly drawnandquarterly.com

COURTNEY CRUMRIN IN THE TWILIGHT KINGDOM

by Ted Naifeh. Courtney Crumrin in the Twilight Kingdom is ™ and © 2003, 2004 Ted Naifeh. Unless otherwise specified, all other material © 2004 Oni Press, Inc. All Rights Reserved. www.onipress.com

D

DEMO

Copyright © 2004 Brian Wood and Becky Cloonan. All Rights Reserved. Published by AiT/Planet Lar. ait-planetlar.com/

DOC FRANKENSTEIN

by the Wachowski Brothers, Steve Skroce, Jason Keith, Comicraft. Copyright © 2004 Burlyman Entertainment, Inc. All Rights Reserved. Published by Burlyman Entertainment. burlymanentertainment.com/

DOGS AND WATER

All contents are © 2004 by Anders Brekhus Nilsen and Airplane. Published by Drawn and Quarterly.

E

EIGHTBALL

by Dan Clowes, 2004 A.D. All Contents © Daniel G. Clowes. All Rights Published by Fantagraphics Books, Inc.

EX MACHINA: THE FIRST HUNDRED DAYS

Ex Machina is ™ Brian K. Vaughan and Tony Harris. All Rights Reserved. Published by WildStorm Productions, an imprint of DC Comics.

F

FABLES: MARCH OF THE WOODEN SOLDIERS

Fables © Bill Willingham and DC Comics. All Rights Reserved. Published by DC Comics/Vertigo

FAMILY REUNION

'Will Kennedy' and 'Family Reunion' are © Sean Stewart. Art © Steve Lieber. seanstewart.org/; www.stevelieber.com Originally published by Small Beer Press: www.lcrw.net/seanstewart

FAREWELL, GEORGIA: FOUR FOLKTALES TOLD BY BEN TOWLE

Farewell, Georgia is ™ and © Ben Towle, all rights reserved. August 2003. Published by Slave Labor Graphics Publishing.

THE FILTH

Copyright © 2002, 2003 Grant Morrison and Chris Weston. All Rights Reserved. Published by DC Comics/Vertigo

FINDER: THE RESCUERS PART THREE

All contents and character likenesses © Carla Speed McNeil. Published by Light Speed Press www.lightspeedpress.com

THE FIXER

by Joe Sacco © 2003 Joe Sacco All Rights Reserved. Published by Drawn & Quarterly

G

THE GOON

by Eric Powell ™ & © 2003 Eric Powell. All Rights Reserved. Published by Dark Horse Comics. www.darkhorse.com/

H

HARD BOILED ANGEL

by Hyun Se Lee English version © 2004 Central Park Media Corp. Published by CPM Manhwa, a division of Central Park Media Corporation. www.centralparkmedia.com/

HSU AND CHAN
™ and © 2004 Jeremy Scott. All Rights Reserved. Published by Slave Labor Graphics

I

IDENTITY CRISIS
© 2004 DC Comics, Inc. Published by DC Comics.

INVINCIBLE
by Robert Kirkman, Ryan Ottley, Bill Crabtree. ™ and © 2004 Robert Kirkman and Cory Walker. All Rights Reserved. Published by Image Comics.

J

JSA ALL-STARS
© 2004 DC Comics, Inc. Published by DC Comics

L

LA PERDIDA
All Contents © 2004 Jessica Abel. Published by Fantagraphics

LAST OF THE INDEPENDENTS
Copyright © 2003 Matt Fraction and Kieron Dwyer. All Rights Reserved. Published by AiT/PlanetLar

THE LEAGUE OF EXTRAORDINARY GENTLEMEN The League of Extraordinary Gentlemen is ™ and © 2003 Alan Moore and Kevin O'Neill. America's Best Comics is ® America's Best Comics, LLC. Cover, design pages and compilation © Alan Moore and Kevin O'Neill.. All Rights Reserved. Published by ABC Comics

LEGENDS FROM DARKWOOD
by Christopher Reid and John Kantz.™ and © 2004 John Kantz and Christopher Reid. All Rights Reserved. Published by Antarctic Press www.antarctic-press.com/

LOVE AND ROCKETS
© 2004 Fantagraphics Books. Individual stories are © 2004 Gilbert Hernandez, Jaime Hernandez, and Mario Hernandez Published quarterly by Fantagraphics Books, Inc.

M

MARVEL 1602
by Neil Gaiman, Andy Kubert, Richard Isanove, Todd Klein covers by Scott McKowen © 2004 Marvel Characters, Inc. Published by Marvel Comics, a division of Marvel Entertainment Group, Inc.

MEGATOKYO
by Fred Gallagher and Rodney Caston ©2004 Fred Gallagher. All Rights Reserved. Published by Dark Horse Comics.

N

THE NEW FRONTIER
© 2004 DC Comics, Inc. Published by DC Comics

NAMBUL WAR STORIES
by Hyun Se Lee. English version © 2004 Central Park Media Corp. Published by CPM Manhwa, a division of Central Park Media Corporation.

NAUSICAA
by Hayao Miyazaki New and adapted artwork and text ©2004 VIZ, LLC. All Rights Reserved. Published by VIZ www.viz.com/

NEOTOPIA
by Rod Espinosa Neotopia and all related characters are ™ and © Rod Espinosa. All other material is ™ and © Antarctic Press. All rights reserved.

NIGHMARES & FAMILY TALES
By Serena Valentino & FSc Nightmares & Fairy Tales is ™ and © 2002-2004, Serena Valentino and FSc. All Rights Reserved.

NINETY CANDLES
© 2004 Neil Kleid Written and illustrated by Neil Kleid Published in conjunction with the Xeric Foundation and Rant Comics. www.rantcomics.com/

O

OJINGOGO
© 2004 Matthew Forsythe Found online at www.onjingogo.com

OPTIC NERVE
by Adrian Tomine © 2004 Adrian Tomine. All Rights Reserved. Published by Drawn & Quarterly

THE ORIGINALS
© 2004 Dave Gibbons All Rights Reserved. Published by DC Comics/Vertigo

OWLY
© 2004 Andy Runton Published by Top Shelf Productions, Brett Warnock and Chris Staros. All Rights Reserved.

P

PERSEPOLIS
by Marjane Satrapi © 2004 Marjane Satrapi All Rights Reserved Published by Pantheon a division of Random House www.randomhouse.com/pantheon/graphicnovels/

PLASTIC MAN
is ™ and © 2004 DC Comics. All Rights Reserved

PRINCESS AI
© 2004 TOKYOPOP Inc. and Kitty Radio, Inc. All rights reserved. Princess Ai is a trademark of TOKYOPOP Inc. and Kitty Radio, Inc. Character designed by Ai Yazawa. Illustrated by Misaho Kujiradou. Published by TokyoPop. www.tokyopop.com/

PROJECT: TELSTAR
Design and AdHouse Logo are © copyright 2003AdHouse Books. "Robot in the Rain" is © copyright 2003 by Paul Rivoche. "We Were Not Made for This World" is © copyright 2003 by Paul Hornschemeier Published by AdHouse Books.

Q

QUEEN & COUNTRY is ™ and © 2003, 2004 Greg Rucka Published by Oni Press, Inc. All Rights Reserved.

R

RAY
by Akihito Yoshitomi ©2003 Akihito Yoshitomi. All Rights Reserved. English text © 2004 Published by A.D. Vision, inc. under exclusive license. ADV Manga is a division of A.D. Vision, Inc. www.adv-manga.com

CREDITS AND COPYRIGHTS

S

THE SANDMAN: ENDLESS NIGHTS
Copyright © 2003 DC Comics. All Rights Reserved. Published by DC Comics/Vertigo

SCANDALOUS
by J. Torres, Scott Chantler ™ and © 2004 J. Torres and Scott Chantler. All Rights Reserved. Published by Oni Press, Inc.

SCOTT PILGRIM SCOTT PILGRIM,
Scott Pilgrim's Precious Little Life ™ & © 2004 Bryan Lee O'Malley. All rights reserved. Published by Oni Press, Inc.

SEAGUY
© 2004 Grant Morrison and Cameron Stewart. All Rights Reserved. Published by DC Comics/Vertigo

SERENITY ROSE
© 2004 Aaron Alexovich. All Rights Reserved. Published by Slave Labor Graphics.

SINGULARITY 7
by Ben Templesmith © 2005 Ben Templesmith and Idea + Design Works, LLC. All Rights Reserved. Published by IDW www.idwpublishing.com

SKYSCRAPERS OF THE MIDWEST
by Joshua Cotter Copyright © Winter 2004. Joshua W. Cotter. Published by Adhouse Books.

SMALL GODS
by Jason Rand, Juan E. Ferreyra, Kristen Simon ™ and © Jason Rand and Juan E. Ferreyra. All Rights Reserved. Published by Image Comics.

SMAX
Cover, design pages and compilation © 2004 America's Best Comics, LLC. All Rights Reserved. Published by ABC Comics.

SPOOKHOUSE
by Scott Hampton © 2004 Scott Hampton. All Rights Reserved. Published by IDW Publishing

STRAY BULLETS
by David Lapham © 2005 David Lapham. All Rights Reserved. Published by El Capitán Books, a division of Lapham, Inc. www.elcapitanbooks.com

STREET ANGEL
™ and © Jimm Rugg and Brian Maruca, 2004, All Rights Reserved. Published by SLG Publishing

SUPERMAN: SECRET IDENTITY
is ™ and © 2004 DC Comics. All Rights Reserved. Published by DC Comics

SUSPENDED IN LANGUAGE
Story © 2003, 2004Jim Ottavianni. Artwork 2003, 2004 Leland Purvis, jay Hosler, Roger Langridge, Steve Leialoha, Linda Medley, and Jeff Parker Published by G.T. Labs (0-9660106-5-5) www.gt-labs.com/

T

TOMMYSAURUS REX
by Doug TenNapel © 2004 Doug TenNapel Published by Image Comics

A TREASURY OF VICTORIAN MURDER: THE BEAST OF CHICAGO
by Rick Geary © 2003 Rick Geary Published by NBM

TSUBASA
by Clamp © Clamp! Studios Published by DelRey Manga a division of Random House Published by Del Rey www.randomhouse.com/delrey/manga/

TWILIGHT X STORM
by Joseph Wight Twilight X and all related characters are ™ and © Joseph Wight and Arclight Pictures International. All othe Materials is ™ and © 2004 Antarctic Press. All Rights Reserved. Published by Antarctic Press

U

ULTRA
by Jonathan Luna and Joshua Luna ™ and © 2004 Jonathan and Joshua Luna. All Rights Reserved. Published by Image Comics.

W

THE WALKING DEAD
by Robert Kirkman, Tony Moore, Charlie Adlard ™ and © 2004 Robert Kirkman and Tony Moore. All Rights Reserved. Published by Image Comics.

WE3
© 2004 Grant Morrison and Frank Quitely All Rights Reserved. Published by DC Comics/Vertigo

WORLD OF HARTZ
© Terrence Walker and TOKYOPOP Inc. All Rights Reserved. Published by TokyoPop

X

XXXHOLIC
by Clamp © Clamp! Studios Published by DelRey Manga a division of Random House Published by Del Rey

Y

YOSSEL
Copyright © 2003 by Joe Kubert. All Rights Reserved. ibooks, inc.

YOU CAN'T GET THERE FROM HERE
All Characters, stories, and artwork © 2004 Jason. All Rights Reserved. Published by Fantagraphics Books.